Judy

Thanks for th
coffee & th
friendship

Stan

Live Like You Mean It

Live Like You MeanIt

The Exhilaration of Being in Control

Floyd Hurt

Published in the United States
by Arete Communications
920 9½ Street, NE
Charlottesville, VA 22902 USA
www.aretecommunications.com

    Hurt, Floyd.
        Live like you mean it : the exhilaration of being in
    control/ Floyd Hurt.—1st ed.
        p. cm.
        LCCN 2002091057
        ISBN 0-9718416-0-8

        1. Self-actualization (Psychology) 2. Conduct of
    life. 3. Success. I. Title.

BF637.S4H87 2002   155.2'5
                                 QBI02-701521

This book is for my terrific kids, Morgan and Eric.

There is no way I could have hoped for more.

Enjoy every aspect of your life.
It's always up to you.
That's the very best I have to give.

Table of Contents

Acknowledgements

Writing is a solitary endeavor requiring a number of people. Without them, motivation falters, ideas dry up, and the days at the computer are long and unproductive. There are far too many people to thank for help in writing this book. It may have been the solitary lady staring out the window on a tram in Vienna, the delightful man in the Atlanta airport who brought me a pillow as I slept on the floor, the small boy leading a donkey down a back street in Turkey. They are all part of the matrix that goes into writing.

There are a few people I want to thank directly for putting up with me and my errant thoughts. To start, Jill Saperstein. Not only is she a wonderful and critical editor, she is a wonderful life partner. Each morning, each day, each evening is made rich just looking over and seeing her close at hand. It puffs me up and makes me whole.

Next, my sister Laurie Johnston. I have spent my entire life with this woman and she has never ceased to amaze me at her lust for living and her ability to make living better for all those around her. You do exemplify all this book is trying to say. Thanks for the path that helped my way.

My mother, Laurie Hurt, all one could hope for in a guide.

Michelle Reid a patient and insightful editor with an infectious smile that hides a core amazement at how badly I spell. Jim Hennerberry. A man with a gift for questions and an open mind to explore all answers.

The rest, those who passed through in books, and life, opening wonder.

A Consideration

This book is about you. Not everyone. Just you in a very private and singular sense. It's about the shadow hiding behind the "you" everyone sees. This book will ask you to look at parts of who you are and how you live, then determine if some of these parts are truths or various colors and shades of omission, half-truths or direct lies. It will then ask you what experiences you are giving up by living these lies. Tough questions.

The book will provoke. You will not agree with parts. All the better, it means you're thinking. I will make bold, overarching statements that I won't apply to everyone or to every situation. The interesting parts of most things are at the edges, not those things with which everyone agrees. Look for the idea, not the detail. Interpret and reconsider from your unique perspective, but don't let that perspective be a filter that screens out new ideas. Try to be open to the full range of possibilities. Try not to dwell on the exception or pass judgment. That can come later.

Contrary to how some parts of this book may sound, it's a study in truth pursued, not truth possessed. I have no final truth; it's far too elusive. However, every exploration must start somewhere.

I hope this exploration will be difficult for you. I hope it will be as difficult for you to read and consider as it has been for me to write. My process of researching and writing has been one of self-confrontation and self-realization. In mucking about in my head, I recognized that I'm a liar and I miss experiences far too often in my own life.

I was in New York a number of years ago staying at a hotel on Lexington Avenue. I always enjoy looking out the window onto the streets of this city. That day was no exception. In the hotel across the street was a very attractive woman polishing her boots. The unusual aspect to the polishing was that she had on no clothes. It was a fine spring day so I just thought I would keep looking out the window. I looked, she polished. After about a half-hour of watching and polishing, watching and polishing, she finished. I went to the coffee shop across the street for breakfast. I was at the counter sipping my coffee when I looked down and saw a remarkably well polished pair of boots coming to rest under the stool next to me. I followed the boots up to the owner and was flabbergasted to see a very beautiful (unfortunately) well-dressed woman. She looked at me, I looked at her. Now I knew as she was polishing that she knew someone(s) was watching her. As she polished, she had made a conscious effort to stand near the window delectably twisting and turning to attract and reflect the best light. So, here I am not one foot away. Okay, what to do? I turned back to my coffee, finished my eggs, paid my check and left. As I headed out the door I discovered at least three new ways to kick myself in the butt for not having the guts to strike up a conversation with someone with whom I had recently been so intimate. Really, how tough is "nice boots?" A missed experience.

I also came to understand that many of the compromises I live with and the excuses I make for doing or not doing something are within my control and it's ridiculous to delude myself into thinking I have no choice. There is always another choice.

Always.

If I choose not to execute an interesting choice for fear of judgment or fear of failing, I slip into resentment, which I then try to displace onto others. With enough of these slippages, resentment becomes a way of life and I find new ways to blame others for my shortcomings and insufficiencies.

Resentment is always about you, never about the actions of

someone else. It's always about *you* and the way *you* feel about what *you* did or did not do in a given situation. Example, you resent your husband because he expects you to be home every night at six o'clock fixing dinner, regardless of any of your other obligations. Really? You resent him? Perhaps what you really resent is your own impotence in not setting boundaries and establishing the kind of expectations and responsibilities that are fair to both. You are mad at him because of something you failed to do.

My insight into resentment revealed a perspective that forced me to take full responsibility for myself, and precluded displacing my self-deception onto others. This awareness has proven both liberating and challenging. As you read, I hope you will discover the same duality for yourself.

Chapter 1
A Commitment

Why this book?

Because life is complex and hectic. Because we seldom, if ever, just sit back and look at where we are and decide if we are in control or just on the ride. Because we often just go along with conditions as they are, not stopping to see if these conditions add dimension to our life or narrow it. It's in this "adding of dimension" that one finds life to be a journey worth taking. Also, because life is short!

So, in a sentence, this book is written "to help you make the conditions for the possibility of a damn great life." What you do with these conditions and this life no one can tell you. That's entirely up to you. It's your life. You are responsible for it. It's always your decision.

Before you start your journey of reading, commit to achieving a complex and impossible goal: purge your past. Get rid of your history and all the baggage holding you down. Pretend there is nothing dictating or directing your life. No beliefs, no "obligations," no responsibilities, no dad, no mom, no church, no school. From this make-believe vantage point, everything is possible, everything is new, nothing is prohibited. To give pulse, breath, and life to this idea imagine you are plopped down on an island about which you know nothing. You have no information or understanding of culture, beliefs, or rituals of the people who live here. On this island every belief is new, accepted, and open for exploration. There are no norms or generally accepted modes of behavior. The only recognized questions: Is it true? Does it work? Nothing is a given. Nothing is set in stone. You are free. Within this personal *tabula rasa,* all the different shades of lies with which you have been living vanish. You are no longer restricted by what could be an antiquated belief system.

Although clearly impossible, this adventure allows your mind to play in a unique field of fantasy, capriciously moving from speculation to speculation with no self-imposed restrictions. Indeed, you'll learn as you proceed that the preponderance of restrictions in lives are ultimately self-imposed. All new thinking and new actions are the children of fantasy. A fantasy that sits just outside the day-to-day you. For just these few pages, give your fanciful potential unrestricted room to fly. You'll be amazed at the highs you can hit without all that "stuff" holding you earthbound.

A word of prudence. If you are not ready to question and examine who you are, what you do, why you do it, what you believe and why you believe it, put this book away; better yet give it away. The void you'll be looking into may be too deep. This book is not for you.

It may be later.

What you'll be asked, at a minimum, is to question beliefs, "givens" and actions. You'll be challenged to abandon your inauthentic self to the authentic self. In accepting the challenge, you'll discover a superior you to the one under the lock-and-key of "it's the way everyone does it, therefore it must be right!" Man will never fly, the earth is flat, a man on the moon? Right! the earth is the center of the universe. In this new space you'll view the world through clean windows, un-smudged and un-streaked with the grime and pollution of dubious rituals, misguided beliefs and arbitrary proscriptions.

If you choose to embark on this journey, you'll find yourself adrift. I know I did. Where you'll travel, the landmarks are unfamiliar. You may end up traveling alone for some time. You'll find tremendous resistance, counter-productivity, hostility, and rejection as you reach out into new territory. You'll be asking the people around you to change the way they perceive you—at best this may seem threatening to them; at worst, alienating. I have a close friend who spent a fuzzy block of his life as an alcoholic. The day he walked into a AA meeting his friends walked out of his life. He had alienated them by taking control of his life and they did not want any part of it. He lost nothing.

The more rejection you encounter, the more difficult it will be to maintain your resolve. There is little we fear more than being alone or rejected. Remember, you have taught people how to treat you and now you are asking them to change and accept a new understanding of the way you now act and think.

Herculean.

In the following pages there will be jargon. Minimal. There is, however, one specific word/concept that, because of its central importance, requires some introduction: "proscribed." The concept surrounding this word is fundamental to this book. I have tried to form a clear understanding of the word, but it remains elusive. The one synonym I find most accurate is "restricted." By extension, I have written this book around the following statement/idea:

> *You are proscribed when you are no longer "allowed"*
> *to have the kind of experiences you want, or when you*
> *lower your level of expectations to accommodate what*
> *is "allowed," never questioning, acknowledging, or*
> *realizing that you are doing so, or that you have a*
> *choice not to. You are proscribed when you have aban-*
> *doned the authentic you.*

Don't take this idea to the extreme. I'm not so naive as to believe that we are not all proscribed by society, by choice and by design in thousands of ways. We live in a world with others. We breathe. We must make allowances. If we were not proscribed, we could choose not to stop at stop lights, we could choose not to take care of our children, we could steal at will and with no consequences. Most of the time it serves us well to choose to go along. The distinction, however, between having to breathe and having a choice to believe or not to believe in things that limit your growth is the crux of this book. If you find yourself acquiescing or always giving in to "keep the peace," or because you "have no choice," then you are not free. You have abdicated your responsibility to yourself. You are proscribed. Chances are, your life is taking on a dull hue.

As the awareness of your personal responsibility grows, a new dimension of freedom slips in like an uninvited guest. You must now, conceptually or factually, move from one system of truth and understanding to another. As you stake out new territory, be prepared. There is no guarantee that this new system of subjective truth will prove any better. Quite possibly, especially at first, it will seem much worse, like chafing new boots that take some time to break in. You may even decide (everything is a decision) to regret abandoning the tried and true.

Therein lurks the risk.

Therein lies the adventure.

Growth is its own reward.

The challenge of all this is to become the kind of person you envision in moments of introspection, the one who does not deceive him or herself. Who doesn't make excuses that he knows are lies. Who doesn't accept beliefs and dogmas because they are told or extorted. The kind of person keenly aware that we must have a wide and varied range of experiences, or we'll never fully know what it means to walk the blue green planet and be a conscious being.

A growing person.

Additional prudence. If you are not committed to acting on your new insights, and are reading only as an academic endeavor, ask why. The playing field is already far too crowded and littered with people who stand on the field, watch and never play the game. There is only one final truth—our actions. The turf on the field of play is never kicked up by spectators, only players. Your actions and your passions alone differentiate you from the rest, and accepting the consequences of your actions is the price of admission onto the playing field. To act is to be, to be is to act.

True simplicity. True difficulty.

Now, contrary to how all this may sound, this book is not about living in a world free from all lies. In many ways lies lubricate society. We all live with lies of omission, white lies that keep someone's feelings from being hurt. Lies like these are a given, unchangeable part of human existence and of any working society. Most often these lies have little impact on our daily life.

I'm talking about lies that proscribe and prevent growth. Lies that are life-denying. The tough kind:

- My wife hates country music, so I gave it up.
- I'm not good enough to write a book.
- I would love to go tieless, but . . .
- I have to, it's for the kids.
- I'm gay, I have to hide it.
- I have no choice, I'll go to hell.
- It's what everybody does.
- What will the neighbors say?
- There is nothing I can do.

It's not a lie to consciously pursue ideas and activities that gratify you, enhance your life, magnify your existence, and have as little negative impact as possible. It's the hallmark of a fully functioning human.

In a Disneyesque society full of spectators eager to accuse the individual thinker of selfishness, far too many of us abandon personally important beliefs, goals, actions, even our sexuality, because we can't stand the fire, brutality, and razor cuts of judgment. We learn to lie, retreat, abandon. With this abandonment comes a host of maladies: hostility grows, depression insinuates, (millions of prescriptions for anti-depressants a year) creativity slips, individual initiative becomes conformity, and uniformity becomes the rule. We all start believing our lies about how great it is to drive the "right" car, wear the "right" clothes, live in the "right" house, believe in God, and never, never, never rock the boat. We become subservient to symbols. During all of this we find ourselves baffled and disoriented by a gnawing feeling that we have given up a huge hunk of who we are in hopes of not being excommunicated or labeled selfish.

Ah, yes! Selfishness.

To liberate the person you are is not an act of selfishness. It is a supreme act of authenticity. If you are accused of being selfish for reaching out and attempting to grow, question the selfishness of the accuser. Exactly who is being selfish? You or they?

Isn't their request that you not change also a selfish request? So, where's the difference? You change, you're being selfish. You don't change, they're being selfish.

To champion others to live with their self-destructive lies by telling them they have "no other choice," or that they are not "responsible," is a hideous form of power and counter productivity. Sanctioning these lies helps bind that person to a fiery wheel of self-deception that scorches growth and discourages a search for new ways of solving problems and expanding horizons. It serves no one.

Before you proceed, and as you proceed, know that the quest for the authentic you is the voyage that makes life a delightful adventure—an adventure that stops only at the end. I knew a powerful, hard-nosed, hard-driving businessman named George. At retirement, he radically changed into a wandering, footloose, nature lover. His whole life was about growth and seeking new adventures. At no point did he think there was nothing more to do or learn. To this man, every day was unique and the final punctuation mark would not be made till the very end. At that end point it could be said "this was George," but until that end point there was only the story of an amorphous George. His final definition was still up in the air.

If you are alive and defined, you are stagnant.

To make the most of the adventure, ask yourself these questions about the decisions you make in your life:

Are they of my own making?

Are they life-affirming or life-denying?

Are they true?

The choice is yours. After all, it's your life. It's your moment in the great cosmic adventure. You wouldn't want to miss it, would you?

Chapter 2
Sitting and Thinking

India, November 2000

I sat in a Jain temple, a great place to pretend to ponder really big questions. I had no delusion that any of my answers would prove any more correct than the thousand that had preceded me, but they were new to me and perhaps they will be new to you. Who knows?

This temple sits high on a hill overlooking the smokey city of Bombay. The temple is a small place with exquisitely carved marble columns and walls. I positioned myself as far away from the tourists and gawkers as I could, then sat on the cool floor. I was not there for religious reasons. I was there because I liked the ambiance and the notion that it was a place to think. There's so little around today that encourages just sitting and thinking.

Bombay is a city of about twenty million people. It is said that half of them are homeless. Driving in at 2:30 AM and seeing the streets lined with sleeping bodies, I had little doubt that may be true. Sitting on the cool floor, my first thought was about all those people and how they manage to live in relative harmony. I considered that it might be in how they treat each other. My question for consideration then became, how should people treat each other, and is there a correct way to do so?

From there I moved into thinking how one should treat oneself.

To this question there really seems to be but one answer: I

should treat others the way I want to be treated. In a formal, Kantian (one of the all time great, though difficult, philosophers) setting, this is called the Categorical Imperative. In a day-to-day setting it passes as the Golden Rule. As an earth-bound, working ethic, I find it almost perfect. If I define it through the impressive Categorical Imperative, the definition would read something like: "Act so that you would want the basic truths or principles of your actions to become a 'law of nature' applying to everyone." If you thought it was OK to steal, by this Categorical Imperative, it would be OK if everyone else too were a thief. It's a law of nature that you have made. If you don't hold up your end of a contract, then you would be fine with someone not holding up their end of a contract with you. You made the law and now you have to live with it. The short version of this becomes, "do unto others as you would have them do unto you." So far, so good.

With a little more thinking, it suddenly hit me that there's a big hole in this concept. You're sitting in a class with a bunch of other students and the teacher is a hard and fast believer in the Categorical Imperative. What impact would that have on you? He looks out on the smiling faces and says to himself, "If I was in this class, I would want an 'A.' I'll just give everybody an 'A.'" Now, whether you come to class or not, do the homework or not, participate or not, you'll get an "A". To the professor, that's elegantly fair. That's what he would want, he made the law, that's what you get.

But, you work hard for your A, and you don't think it's fair that the guy who doesn't even show up for class also gets an A. You protest to the professor. It has no impact. He believes in the Categorical Imperative without limitations or restriction. What to do?

Take a couple of steps back and consider what you really want from the class. Do you want a grade that is a reflection of the rest of the grades in the class? Do you want to shine and prove you are the smartest? Maybe you want an A so you can graduate with a higher grade point average. In the last case you are delighted to have a professor with such a strong belief in the Categorical Imperative. But the underlying problem is that in all these cases something outside you determines the importance and worth of the class. So what final result do you want from the class? The A to get into grad school is a strategy, not the final result.

At this point in my thinking I hit the wall. Yes, indeed the Categorical Imperative may be the very best ethical way to deal with people, trees, dogs, the air, the land, on a day-to-day basis. It adds a most remarkable clarity and ethical foundation to choice making, and to the treatment of our world in the vast majority of situations. It may be the best we have. It just leaves a slice missing from the pie.

I shifted my position on the cool floor. The afternoon sun reflected on my paper as a tiny green bug crawled across the page. A small, infinitely meaningless and infinitely meaningful citizen of a hot town teeming with people and unsolvable problems.

It was that question of *result* that kept coming back. The result for me. Even if the *result* I wanted from the class was the knowledge, that did not seem to take it far enough. Knowledge to do what and for what reason? That kept haunting me. I know how to fix a flat or use a computer, but so what? Then what? I wanted something bigger, a final result to aim for. A closing of the circle.

About now, I began to wonder if I was simply substituting the word "result" for the word "meaning"? Was I straining with the age-old problem of what's it all about? No, in fact I think there is a big difference between the result of my life and meaning in my life. Result, I figured, was the sum total, a tally of what life should be. At the end of it how would I judge all the tears, laughter, food, new shoes, wind, flu, ball games, and relationships? These judgements and evaluations would constitute the result of my life.

Meaning, on the other hand, is the continuing activities of life. For example, I may find meaning in taking a walk or tending a garden. Meaning attending a wedding or in the birth of a child. It's in the actual doing and day-to-day participation that meaning appears. It is not the end or the terminus point of our life. Once we stop what we are doing and ask what it all means, the meaning is lost in the tumult of the question. To find meaning in life, simply live it and be aware of the things that happen. That's where one finds meaning.

Meaning I understand. Result remains obscure, but I know if I let meaning flow, a result I wanted would follow.

Needless to say, looking for a final result was a jump into a deep existential void. As I felt around in the darkness I noticed thousands who had jumped before. Wonder what they came up with? I also wondered why, after so many years of looking, no one has come up with an answer, or answers, with which we all agree. It is indeed a dark existential void.

I hopped up and walked to the intricately carved balcony overlooking Bombay. My two hours of musing had taken me to the point of wondering about the result one should expect of one's life. It was a vastly interesting and deeply provocative question. It needed an answer.

Night had settled on Bombay. The streets were alive with people. People with no place to go.

Chapter 3
Setting the Stage

Your first challenge: enjoy life.

Your second challenge: take full responsibility for doing so.

These two precepts seemed pivotal keys to answering the question of result.

Who are we? What are we supposed to do? Why do we do the things we do? Why do we choose not to do many things we want? What kind of choices do we have? What kind of choices should we have? Why do we make so many choices that seem to run counter to what we know is true and correct for us?

These vexing and thorny questions haunt all of us from time to time as we wander through our days. For the most part, our choices require little real thinking. We seldom stop to question why we answer the phone, take out the garbage, drive our kids to school. These are just things "everybody" does, and it makes sense to go along, even if sometimes "going along" goes against what we really feel or believe.

But ....

Things can change radically when, for some reason, often late at night, we sit up in bed and look around the dark room and ask ourselves "why"? Why do I feel locked in, or why did I choose this or that course of action when I didn't really want to? Why do I just go along? Why do I sometimes feel such dread and anxiety about things over which I should have control? What essential part of my real existence am I giving up to keep from rocking the boat? How much of life do I miss because of phantom fears and hollow dreads? How much of what I think, feel, believe is not at all of my making but given to me by someone else? When do I let the real me out and become who I am? Is there really such a thing as authenticity?

At this nocturnal point of uncertainty you have two choices.

First option: lie back down, close your eyes and pretend nothing's going on, that there is nothing even to consider. Just lie there and hope the feeling goes away. It won't. No matter how we layer it over with gooey, transparent forgeries of our genuine self, that interruptive feeling is always there. Self-deception is a potent force and, even with all its power you can never fully deceive yourself into believing these large questions about life have no impact on you. But you can try.

This deception won't be new to you. It's ingrained. You've been deceiving yourself for so long about so many things you've forgotten what it's like to know or even search for your personal truth. The realization that you have let that truth slip through your hands like just so much sand may keep you awake for a few minutes, but not long. At this point you have inattentively slipped from quiet desperation into resolved desperation. The trek up the existential hill is far too steep.

Rest. Sleep. There's always the fantasy of next time.

Second option: resolve to change. Resolve that your visit here is of short duration, and the way you choose to live during that remarkable visit is, at every level, your responsibility. Resolve that statements like "I couldn't do anything else, don't you see?" will be replaced by, "I've considered all options, and based on what I know and how I feel, I decided this course is best for me and those around me. I will not ensnare them in my lies." Resolve and accept that the consequences of your choices are yours alone and can never ever be passed off to anyone or anything else.

A wee-hour conversation.

The first option is easy. Just keep doing what you've been doing. It's so easy for people to do, it even has a name: "Flight from Freedom."

The second option requires a fundamental change in the way

you see yourself and the way those around you expect you to be and to behave. Igniting a new order of personal behavior comes only with an awareness of the boundaries you have constructed or allowed to be constructed around you. It also comes with an understanding that not one of these boundaries is built of such enduring stuff that it can't be broken down, rearranged, or completely destroyed.

The onerous and exhilarating challenge is to determine which boundaries are supportive and which limiting. This exercise would be counterproductive if we destroyed all the structures that define us. Who we are, our current authenticity, would be destroyed too. Without them, authenticity eliminates itself. Some boundaries are critical and should be guarded at all costs. Problem is, which ones? Boundaries that seem most helpful may be the most detrimental, and vice versa. Knowing which to question, which to keep, which to modify, and which to eliminate is the task of the growing person.

Total freedom from boundaries is illusory and not the objective. If it were indeed possible, total freedom's sibling would be total estrangement.

Total estrangement precludes participation.

Participation is vitality.

Participation limits freedom.

The freedom circle closes—but only to the degree you choose.

Proceed with caution, consideration, circumspection.

Chapter 4

Washed Up On Shore

To start.

One arbitrary day you washed up on the shore of a time and a place. The color of the sky that first, arbitrary day was as arbitrary as that place and that arbitrary time. Through radical happenstance, you appeared. This chance appearance was initiated and consummated without your consultation and without your permission. At no point during the process did anyone sit you down, discuss options or provide any information about the consequences of appearing at this time and this place. You were a bystander to the events that started the process.

A curious beginning.

Equally curious, the end.

The wind will blow from the east on the last day as randomly as the color of the sky on the first day. You will be at a specific place in a specific time. It could just as easily have been at another place at another time. There will be no consultation, no discussion. The last wave good-bye will fulfill the scheduled departure, closing the circle on the curious journey with as much mystery as the first cry on a sandy beach.

A solitary beginning, a befuddled end, the enigma between.

It is our awareness of the random beginning and the arbitrary end that forces us to give our own form and significance to the enigmatic interlude between. Anything on either end is, at its very, very best, mythology, and only a gullible optimist would sacrifice the known time for a fabricated promise of pie-in-the-sky-by-n-by.

14

The critical consideration: outside shady, suspect, and simplistic religious beliefs, to the very best of our unqualified knowledge and understanding, when and where you appeared was an unhampered roll of the cosmic dice. You exist now, not then. You are here not there. Given a minor, random shift of any natural events, there would be no you to wash up. Given the same arbitrary toss, your accidental cat would not be sitting in the equally random window on a unique rock ninety-three million miles from an undistinguished ball of fire. It is all fortuitous. But the haphazard progression of events and chance fell your way, and here you are, no more unique than the cat, window, ball of fire.

The luck of it all!

The reality of it all....

Ascribing any absolute importance to when and where you wash up or wave good-bye is an act of absurd hubris. Random is random, and any hoping that it is more than random and full of meaning or significance is just that...hoping. In this knowledge, any defense of temporal or geographic norms and absolutes must be relegated to dust, swept away in the breezes and hurricanes of time, unanchored on the randomly roving tectonic plates of kings, wars and inventions. Random is the flow of history.

Imagine you were born in another time and another place. All the standards of behavior and beliefs you defend with gusto today become as vaporous and transient as those of the past. The earth was flat and the center of the universe. The pharaoh was God on earth. To believe that one thing is right and another wrong simply means you were born in a time or place when truth had a different definition.

This doesn't mean you are absolved from living with today's norms. No one is. It just means that these norms may be loaded with flaws and that every norm should be open to examination and question. There are no moral "facts." There are only temporal and geographic interpretations of facts. Things change.

So, who would you be in another time or at another place? Not "you." What would be your belief system? Not one of the 21st century.

A deep understanding of this concept opens a window to vast fields of non-judgmental opportunities. Just because you are a product of your own time does not mean you are right and the past was wrong. In fact, that which seems right today will surely be wrong in another time or place. Dogmatically defending or condemning our time forces limited participation. Limited experience.

So, there you are standing alone on a long stretch of sandy beach in a land and time about which you have no knowledge and no experience. Your "givens" at this point in your existence are clear: a person, five senses, breathing, digesting food ...outside of this you know nothing about this place and time into which you have been catapulted. You have no clue about what to do, how to act, what words mean, how others will view you, how you'll view others, or what you'll need to accept and reject as you move off your sandy beach. You are little different from the rock you sit on, contemplating this alien time and this alien place. The rock, too, has no notion of why it rests on the shore or what it's there to do. The significant difference is that you are aware you don't know and you're asking the question; the rock isn't.

Consciousness and self-consciousness have entered your vista. You question.

What's to be learned and remembered?

First, you have a single-sided contract with the world. It owes you nothing. To nature, you owe survival. To biology, you owe reproduction. From this impersonal vantage point, if you fail to survive and fail to duplicate yourself as many times as you can, you have missed your calling, simply taken up space, and have no reason to be. You are disposable.

Second, aside from that simple task of procreation, what you do with your unrevealed and unnumbered days is up to you. The earth and nature have no interest or care. That's your responsibility.

Chapter 5
Enter the Map-makers

It's time to leave the sandy beach. But by what course, and in what direction? How do we know which way to go if we arrive adrift, or if reference points are random and have no meaning. Right or left makes no difference. Being lost is simply a matter of having no fixed points of reference… if there are no markers, there can be no maps. Freedom is simply stumbling into a void, and only with stationary points of light or reflected light does the void take shape, gain dimension and become reality.

Here we find the map-makers to help or hurt. Mom, dad, friends, minister, drill sergeants, philosophies, and institutions put markers on our maps. They tell us that these markers are established, fixed parts of the landscape, but the map-makers too were tossed up on a random beach at a random time. They too are temporal and geographical. They don't really know they are fooling us. They were fooled, too. These markers become our givens, providing reference points and guides as we move on our bewildering journey. We are ignorant. We believe. How could we choose not to? Where else could we turn?

With astounding velocity, we are shaped by the boundaries of our maps. Sometimes we are led to believe that dragons dwell at the edges of the map, or that if we stray too close we'll fall off. In truth without many of these landmarks and edges, we would indeed fall into a void where locating ourselves would prove an impossible task. It's through understanding and appreciating these landmarks that we interpret our world and define who we are. They are a necessary part of growth.

Here, too, we begin learning a language. With this knowledge "hot" becomes more than a tactile experience, "eternity" becomes overpowering, "love" becomes meaning, "nigger" and "honky" become demeaning. Through language our landmarks can be expressed and understood. The better our understanding of language, the better our understanding of the world. Words form and express our reality.

In time, though, some of the landmarks seem strangely out of place, ill-fitted with the others. But they have been placed by respected authorities, so we believe them and work around them; covering them over or even modifying them to fit what seems to be the most accepted, least disturbing, least disruptive, more prudent path to follow. Reinforcement, fear, manipulation, and extortion by those we trust forces us to work hard turning abstract, confusing landmarks into an understandable reality. "That's a good little girl," "It's the way we do it here in this class," "If you don't believe, you'll go to hell," "Santa won't bring you anything," "Daddy loves you, he didn't mean to hit you, he was a little drunk." These become markers and signposts on our path that we manipulate and neatly place into what we believe.

Fearing rejection or alienation, our greatest fear, we don't question. Or we are told not to question. The result? Some sections of the path become foggy as we struggle to reconcile what we have been told with what we are seeing and learning from other mapmakers and others stumbling in the void.

It is here, in the map-making stage, that restrictions, truths, half-truths and lies insidiously find a home. The more of the mapmakers' absolute "truths' ("this is *the* truth," "our way of life is the only way," "don't touch yourself there," "those people are sinners") that are heaped upon us at an early stage, the narrower our path. Although we may not overtly be aware of these statements as questionable, we sense growing contradictions between what we see, what we think may be right and the path we are being told to accept and follow. Often, the harder we try to reconcile the confusion by asking questions, the more stringent becomes the punishment and retribution. After enough of these penalties and condemnations, we suppress what we really feel and construct a new reality in strict accordance with the rules.

Lies generally involve consent by both parties. You lie, I accept. You believe I have accepted the lie because I don't call you on it. We are in cahoots.

Without knowing it, we have become proscribed because of how important it seems to us not to break the ties with those we trust, those we fear. Since all of our actions relate to how we feel about something, we are willing, if not compelled to make radical alterations in our perceptions and virgin reality to maintain important relationships, regardless of the consequences. "I will be whatever you need or however you desire me" ... I will fool you, I will fool me.

The genesis and slippery slope of self-deception.

As we move ahead in our lives, we start to construct our own reality using the markers and tools supplied by our map-makers. Each new situation means dipping into this toolbox to see if we can find the right tool for this challenging job of understanding, adapting to and fashioning our own new reality. Because nothing is ever truly analogous to anything else, we began using our tools in unique and creative ways. If the map-maker's influence was open, supportive, and expansive, we are encouraged to use our tools in these new and creative ways.

Exciting variety.

Exhilarating options.

If, on the other hand, our map-maker's domination involved severe prohibitions, absolute rights and wrongs, unconditional goods and evils, despotic gods and devils, we find ourselves battling to make strange situations yield to the rigidity of our tools and the way we were told things are and must be. We commit to denying that there may be other truths, other opinions. We believe that those who feel differently or think differently from ourselves are at best wrong, or at worst deviant. We close ourselves off from alternatives, making excuses, rules, and dogmas to justify ourselves in our narrow cage. We fear stepping beyond the boundaries toward the dragons. Dread takes hold as we fear the wrath of an angry god, the night stalker, or the paranoia that our children will be kidnapped. We impose that fear and trepidation on those around us. We condemn them if they are unwilling to relinquish their liberty when we tell them of the danger, the angry god, the night stalker. We hold them in contempt if they read the wrong book, one that is not sanctioned by the powers that have crafted our map. We know what's right—we are missionaries and there is no questioning.

A mind is a terrible thing to narrow.

Although absent, the autocratic, iron-fisted map-maker threatens and punishes the recalcitrant wanderer. It is safer to give in. We acquiesce.

Even if, at a deep level, we know they don't deserve it, we protect our map-makers, rejecting the possibility that they ever did anything wrong. This defense strengthens our belief in what we have been told. Every time we act on a belief, we add strength to the belief. By defending and justifying, we move deeper and deeper into self-deception, entrenching beliefs, eliminating outside influence, restricting experiences.

The cloister, the monastery, the troop, the golden ghetto.

To achieve a better understanding of where you are on a truth scale, you need a more detached view of your map-maker's intention. This means taking a step back and examining things as impersonally as you can. That's tough. Little is more difficult for a human than to perceive something impersonally; but without some detachment all of our perceptions are filtered through imbedded, pre-conceived notions and prejudices that cloud our understanding.

We're all editors. We have learned what works and what doesn't. It's in this learning that we edit out most things that come our way. This editing allows us to move more smoothly through the day than if each situation required new analysis and novel approaches. On the other hand this knee-jerk editing precludes taking the necessary pause to determine if a unique response to a situation might add dimension and excitement to the day. It also precludes us from taking a step back, away from the internal view of ourselves.

The objective in stepping back is to find a clear view of your world, and decide whether it works for you or against you. From this detached vantage point, you can also stop defending or justifying the parameters the map-maker may have put on your life.

So, pretend you are observing your own life and see how it looks.

Perhaps the best way to start this process is to assume your map-makers had only the best intentions (a good will, as it were) when they marked your path. Maybe it was the way your map-maker's own path was marked that kept him from knowing any other way to mark yours. With this starting point, it's much easier to get over or around the idea that "they done you wrong." This attitude also allows you to make allowances for how things are, and not point fingers at situations and people that have long passed, or should pass, from your sphere of influence.

The next step is to understand that for all of us history is history, and nothing can ever change it. The more we belabor how we got here, the less we can focus on moving in a new direction, and the more we also entrench our feeling of being a victim. In no way does this absolve evildoers with bad intentions. People do bad things, 'tis true, and bad things leave abrasions and scars. Some very deep.

The quandary: to re-frame by taking control and assigning no *negative* value to the act. Or taking control, by not spending any of your time in blame, accusation, and getting even. Failing this, they are in control. You are a bystander, spiraling deep into a gloomy vortex with no bottom; and they don't even know it. They don't care, or if they do, you still allowed them into your life. You deserve them. Re-frame and you dictate. You take control. Address the issues. Process them then let them go if you can. If you can't, get help. Don't become a victim. It has no merit or usefulness.

The outgrowth of this feeling of victimization is a bogus belief that we are owed something for all we went through. Rubbish! Rubbish and again rubbish! None of us is owed anything, and if we think we are, we will dwell in a state of permanent incompleteness. The second we admit to being an ongoing victim, we look for pity, and pity feeds upon itself. Others feed upon the pitiful because they are perceived as inferior. Being pitiful is the last resort of the power-less. Victims seek other victims for confirmation of their pathetic position. They find them. They reinforce each other. The world passed them by. The mill grinds them into a pulp. They disappear. Let history be a guide, never an anchor.

The last step is to know that we can change the way we interpret and deal with this history. Although this will not change what went before, it will change our attachment to these flawed landmark events. We will find in this objective point of view clearer understanding that what went before is simply a prelude. We can take charge of our lives right now. We are in command, and we can choose to choose.

The past has no accountability for who we are and what we do today. With the past as prelude, we are now able to be free. We can re-construct and re-fashion our map and our meaning with our own hands. If we decide not to strike out past the boundaries of our inherited map, that is a choice for which we must take full responsibility. We can't blame someone else; we have made that decision and we will live with the result, no one else. Every passive or active acceptance, every active or passive rejection, is ours. It can't be any other way. The best we can hope for from the outside world is that it will not stand in our way.

That is far too much to expect.

Work for it.

You wash up only once.

Courage.

Chapter 6

The Price of Consciousness

In the quest for *result*, I ran into the mystery of consciousness. Not the question of how one comes to have it, that's not important. What is its relative value in the result I expect of my life? Is it there to help or hurt?

Everything has a price.

Price means the sacrifice of one thing for something else.

Everything has a value.

Value is the importance or worth of the thing for which you have paid a price.

Everything has a cost.

Cost is determined by whether or how much the value of something exceeds the price you paid for it.

A ten dollar frying pan used once has a very high cost. Use it five hundred times and the cost virtually goes away.

Losing a couple of hours of sleep in the morning to go to the gym and exercise is the price one pays to be healthy. The value of being healthy has no limit. The value of the exercise program therefore so exceeds the price that there is no cost at all. To those who "just can't get up," or "just can't find the time for exercise," the cost will be exceedingly high.

Years ago on Coney Island there was a rollercoaster called the Cyclone. It was a huge old wooden structure that rumbled and creaked as the cars careened around the curves and leaped up and down in the bumps and dips. It still stands. The clamor and rattle are lost in the winds of neglect and decay. To experience the ride, folks would sacrifice money… the price of the ride. You knew the price, you paid your money, you got on. There was anticipation, but no grumbling about the price, once you were being hauled up the first drop. You were well aware of the choice you had made, and to flood yourself with questions about the meaning or dread of the ride would have only diminished your enjoyment. In fact, there was no meaning other than the ride itself; the price was just a given.

As you were slammed side to side, the degree to which you enjoyed the ride became the value of the ride. If the first drop snapped your face into an idiotic grin and each hump was an adventure, the value of the ride was high. If you spent the entire ride fretting, eyes closed, tight fisted, fearing the worst and regretting your decision, there was probably no value. In the former case, the actual cost of the ride was low because you got much more value for what you spent… your money's worth. In the latter case, the cost was high because you got little, if any value. In short, the return on your investment sucked.

High value, low cost. Low value, high cost.

Although we washed up on shore through no choice of our own, we now find ourselves conscious of the world. We look around, and as things happen our senses tell us that we are a part of all this wonderful calliope of sounds and tastes and smells and feelings and sights. We savor exceptional food and our awareness of it sends us into a frenzy of delight. We stick our toe in a mountain stream and shiver. We make hot sticky love on a sweltering summer afternoon and then wallow in remembrance. We stand on a hill watching a sunset, fully engrossed in the beauty and wonder of it all.

Awareness… the highest order of existence.

But then, just as the sun sets and the night sky envelops us in inscrutability, we are flooded with an overwhelming sense of confusion. What does it all mean? Why am I here? Where did I come from? What will happen after I die? Was I nice enough to my mom and dad? Will my kids be all right? How long do I have? With those questions, the joy of the sunset, the taste of the food, the steamy sex on a lazy hot afternoon are all overshadowed with perplexity and eerie tumult. The longer we stand on the darkened hill wondering, the more confusing it becomes. We try to find answers. None come. All our lives we try to find the answers. None come. Perhaps, like our ancestors, we construct make believe answers or accept bogus and temporal "understandings" that hold the feelings at bay, but there is always an undercurrent of questioning that's never stilled. The answers we make or accept always have holes, and "facts" leak out as we try to plug the holes with belief piled on belief then belief chiseled into dogma. We want so badly to find an answer. We want so badly to know, that we lie (or settle for lies).

We lie because deep inside we know we can't know all or even a very few answers.

In wanting so badly to know, we accept anything that sounds like an answer. Any answer is better than no answer and we are willing to relinquish a great deal of our humanity in hopes of enlightenment. We build monuments to our wish. On some level we believe if we just build enough or just build these monuments large enough, an answer will emerge and we will have a right and shining understanding.

It doesn't happen. No transcending answers come from the top of the blistering Pyramids, the vine-covered temple at Angkor Wat, the fog-covered mountain of Machu Picchu, or the echoing walls of the National Cathedral. The quest is fruitless.

So what? What's the point of knowing? Would it make a whit of difference if you knew? What would you do differently? Most likely, nothing. Things would go on just about the same. You would fill your days with the same stuff, go to the movie, walk on the sandy beach, aimlessly talk to your friends. You just wouldn't be stuck on a "why."

But you don't know, do you? And you never will. The "why" lingers deep in a night sky sparkling with stars and obscurity.

So how do you accommodate this night-time, top of a hill apprehensiveness? How do you come to grips with the anxiety, fear, dread, lack of meaning, absurdity of it all in your quest for *result*?

Easy answer, tough execution: Accept the price, increase the value, reduce the cost.

The first step. Understand that the door to all the wonderful things that day-to-day consciousness allows you to experience also opens another door at the dark end of the hall. Without full consciousness of the sensual world of human life, you would have no consciousness of your lack of understanding of the mystifying nighttime sky, and the darkness at the other end of the hall. If you were a potato or a tree, the awareness of the soft touch or the jubilant bell would not be part of your existence; but neither would the fact that you will someday cease being a potato or a tree, or that the dark night holds no answers.

The price for an understanding of a sensual touch or a melodic bell is the awareness that there is no answer to your deepest questions.

Take a second to think about this. The tree, the cat, the worm, the chimp all have an awareness of their world. Shine a light on a tree and it will grow toward the light. Pop the top to a cat food can and the feline rush is on. But that's mostly where it stops. Sure, a cat will curl up on your lap or lie in the warmth of the sun, but, to the best of our knowledge, life is not an interpretive experience for the cat. The cat, worm, chimp don't delight in the flood of feelings the sound of thunder brings on a warm summer day. It's just a fact, and something often to be avoided. Animals have awareness but no consciousness of the aesthetics that human beings bring to a situation. Nor do they ponder the bigger questions. Their consciousness limits them on both ends.

As mentioned before, you have a single-sided contract with the world: to nature, survival, to biology, reproduction. But to Being, your own special Being in the world, you owe aesthetic consciousness and creative action. Without that you dwell at the periphery of humanity, never viewing the full spectrum of colors that awareness offers.

But, the price one pays for aesthetic, human consciousness is anxiety, fear, dread, lack of meaning, and the absurdity of it all... and that's OK. The second we realize that it's just a price, the easier it is to enjoy the ride and stop the white-knuckled quest for meaning and the search for some greater force or thing to which we can surrender ourselves. If we are always focused on the price of life, the value is low and the cost is outrageous.

In searching for this value, think of value, in very broad and loose terms of value as a unique kind of bank account. At birth we are all given something we will call "pleasure units." Let's say we get a hundred of them. We can add to these both in quantity and magnitude anytime we want. We are also given a hundred "dread units," things we fear, things that overpower us, things that keep us up at night. We cannot ever add to these, they're fixed in number, but like "pleasure units" they vary in magnitude. Because none of us can avoid the melancholic questioning of meaning, or wallowing in the angst of existence, or fearing for our health and wealth, we will spend our "dread units" at various times and often in the damnedest places. Sometimes that expenditure will be so overwhelming and last so long that we withdraw into a shadowy place of our own. Other times really feeling and tasting one of these dread units may turn into an adventure in itself; an adventure that should not be missed at any cost. There is special excitement in a cosmic mystery if we allow it to become an interesting exercise in coping and wondering, as opposed to a tumble into its oppression...a choice you can often make. But in general, dread units are the confusion and frustration of fearing and not knowing.

Our pleasure units, on the other hand, will be spent on the kind of life experiences we allow ourselves to have. If you go for the brass ring every time it comes around and don't let most things arrest your development, you add to your pleasure units in massive numbers. Each pleasure unit past the one hundred mark nibbles away at the dread units by diminishing their relative worth. In the end, if you had a life filled with tons of experience units, more than likely it was a life worth living.

In this strange "bank account" system, if your life was just OK, you will have had about one hundred pleasure units and about one hundred dread units. This means you worried about dreadful things to about the same degree that you delighted in your experiences. If your life was filled with overpowering guilt, fear, dread, anxiety, and angst, most likely you didn't spend your full one hundred pleasure units, and were limited in the type of and magnitude of experiences you allowed yourself to have. "Fly? Oh, no, the plane might go down." "You can't dress like that, what would the neighbors say?" "I know it's none of my business, but I can't believe he's a homo-sexual. Disgusting!" You get the idea.

Your dread units close doors. The cost is very high. Regret creeps in. Regret? About what?

About all of these self-imposed limitations and fears you choose. Regret is awareness that comes too late...regret is always ex post facto. Most often the regret sneaks in when defenses are down...maybe at a movie during a scene depicting something you always wanted to do. Or in a conversation with an enlightened friend who has both feet in the shifting stream of life. It's at that time that you know, on a gut level, that you passed up a chance to live because of dubious self-imposed limitations. Your judgment was off because of some unquestioned edict a map-maker gave you a long time ago. Judgment failed because you found truth in the "facts" unremittingly pounded into you by TV, radio, newspapers, etc. You lost perspective and never questioned. Then it happened ... You missed your daughter's wedding in Europe because you feared flying.... why? The media scared you. You abandoned your son because his religious or sexual beliefs were not the ones you tried to "ram down his throat". Who won? Who lost? It was his life...now you know. You spent 30 years trying to get back at that son-of-a-bitch for divorcing you. All that time, all that effort and now, noth-ing, just bitterness and missed experiences. You wash your hands every time you touch something. But everybody says germs are bad. Only a fool believes what "they" say, and you know it. You were never sexual because of a night of passion in the back seat of a Ford, a mortal sin. Who told you that? A celibate? You did not have the courage to tell them, "go to hell, you ignorant bastards!" So, you condemned yourself.... you don't need a vengeful god, you do just fine on your own.

You forgot the value and focused on the price.

In my life I never regret the things I've done, only the things I didn't do. A personal story about price, value, cost.

Helen.

Athens.

I was heading home after hitchhiking across equatorial Africa. I flew from Kinshasa to Athens and planned to stay there for a few days before heading to London, then home. The second night I went down to the bar in the small hotel. The room was dim. On the far side was perhaps one of the most beautiful women I had ever seen. Spending three months alone in Africa may have colored my perception somewhat, but I don't think so. I pulled up a stool and introduced myself. She was from Australia and indeed, even without the long solo trip, she was beautiful. We talked for hours about what we had been doing, swapping tales of the road. Everything about her was alive and attractive. She had red hair, bright eyes. A delicious feast. About two in the morning we bid adieu with a plan for dinner the next night.

At seven in the morning the phone rang. It was Helen asking if I wanted to go to the Acropolis. Twist my arm.

The day was perfect. Small white clouds dotted the Greco-blue sky. An ancient breeze eased in from a lost antiquity. We wandered from one myth to another as the day burned its image on a host of neurons.

Dinner in Plaka. We talked, lost among the rainbow of colored lights, balalaikas, cats, and retsina.

"Let's go to the out islands," she said. "We can leave tomorrow morning. I'll come by and get you."

Four A.M. came early and the knock on the door was a bit more than I was ready for. "Come on," she said, "we have to be at the boat in an hour."

And now for a true regret in my life.

"I'm tired, I think I'll pass."

She looked at me as if I had lost my mind. I had. "Okay, I'll be back this afternoon. Want to have dinner?"

"Great."

She left to take the trip alone.

That afternoon some bad weather set in and she couldn't get back. I had to leave the next afternoon.

I never saw her again.

Opportunity is a whimsical gremlin. It sometimes stands there at the door banging away and you have no idea what all the noise is about. Other times it stares you in the face and the best you can muster is: "hey, you look'n at me?" It seldom comes in a wrapping that is so obvious that you know it's talking to you. Helen, Athens, and the warm breeze off the Aegean was a clear opportunity that I just let slip away.

To this day I never say, "I'm tired."

To this day I can't believe I let that day and those warm nights walk away. All that's left is a flashing, point finger that says: "Stupid," flash, "Stupid," flash, "Stupid" flash.

The price of the trip with Helen was getting my butt out of bed. I didn't do it. The cost was so high it stands as a beacon that lights my way to always, always, always understand the value of something as opposed to the price.

AND NOW TO WHINE A BIT

"But I didn't choose to be here, and the price is too high and I don't want to play."

So what? Listen to yourself. What price is too high? Everybody has the same price. Of course you didn't choose to be here, none of us did. But you're focusing on the wrong end of your potential. The price has nothing to do with how you play the game. It's the cost. If you add value, you reduce the cost. If you add no value, the cost is high and you start to "resent" those around you who seem to have little regard for the price, and who continually add value to the way they live.

•

A note about resentment.

Not the English word resentment, but rather the French word *ressentiment*. There is big difference. In English, the word explains a feeling toward someone. "I resent her for what she said to me." The French word explains a feeling toward ones self. "When she said something to me that I didn't like, I didn't have the guts to say anything back or stand up for myself, so *I resent me*, myself, and my lack of courage."

Resentment is always about you, never about someone else.
If you understand this significant difference, you will gain a new awareness of your accusations of someone else. If you resent someone for presenting a new concept (one you may have had) in a meeting, hold up a mirror to yourself and ask who you really resent. Watch for resentment in you and in others... *resentment* is always about the person doing the resenting. According to Nietzsche, it is also the origin of a couple of religions:

The Hebrews manifested their resentment by inventing a wrathful and retaliatory god. This god would punish the tyrannical Romans in the afterlife because the Hebrews could not punish or rebel against them in this life. The best they could do; fabricate an arm's length disciplinarian with total power who would right all the wrongs done to them on earth. Their transparent proclamation of resentment: "We can't. We are feeble. He will even the score."

Later, the Christians broadened this resentment by enhancing the mythology to include a superior and dazzling afterlife. The bad would be excluded from this life and the tormented Christians would be included. For the bad, the mythology dug deep into the sulfurous earth and exposed an unendurable place of fire and endless punishment into which the evil would be cast. Again, "We can't. We are feeble. He will even the score."

Resentment: a diabolical motivator and a surreptitious and conspiratorial creator of history.

•

Another way to avoid playing this game of living is to zonk out your consciousness with drugs...controlled or uncontrolled...and this includes alcohol. More and more people today decide to take that path. Our world is full of folks who can't stand the least bit of angst, so they pop a pill, take a drink, or shoot up. But why? Because they can't come to grips with the simple fact that all the questions, emotions, anxieties, fears, and dreads are just part of the landscape. They've always been and everyone has them; they mean nothing, and are simply the price to enter the game, that's it. If you give over the potential of experience to the life-denying stupor of drugs or alcohol, the cost is far too high. At some point you'll come down, and when you do all the demons that you have kept at bay will be waiting at the gate and will come crashing in on you in overwhelming numbers. You'll retreat back to the poppy, the hops, the weed. All will be lost. At this point you won't recognize the loss because you've checked out; the stupor becomes more and more inviting, letting in fewer true experiences in hopes of keeping at bay the demons lurking outside the bottle.

You have jettisoned your life and all the adventures that travel with it. You are a drain on yourself and those around you. If they let you into their world, they deserve you and the evil abuse that tags along with you. If you force your way in, you deserve to be set adrift in a small leaky boat on a tempestuous and unforgiving sea on a frozen night. Stay away.

If you work hard to keep the cost low, the stupor has little appeal. If you confuse the stupor with an adventure, then at the come-down point the hard realization that so much has been lost will enter like a barbarian coming to pillage all remaining physical and mental health. There may be no recovery.

And yet another way to avoid the price is to hide from it by embracing a deep and unreasoned belief in something outside yourself that you think holds the "answer." The key word here is "unreasoned." To give yourself over to belief out of fear or because "they" told you it was the "right thing," or because it's written down in a book, or because you were extorted into believing that a hideous consequence awaited you if you did not believe, may seem prudent but it's not true...it's a lie. Buying into an unreasoned belief forces you to deny a host of experiences and to fear a wrathful god. This is a supreme act of self-denial that becomes life-denying and serves to increase the cost of existence.

Review carefully what you believe and why you believe it. This consideration will have a tremendous impact on the *result* you want from your life.

At the end of the game, you will have about the same answers to the big questions as everyone does at the beginning. If you enjoy the seeking and questioning, go for it. If, on the other hand, the quest and the questions become debilitating and life-denying, put them aside. Not to worry, there will be others to take them up. Besides, any answer you come up with would change nothing that you can't change already if you choose.

Chapter 7
And Now for RESULT

The Bombay question remains: "What *result* do you want from your life?" By what criteria will you measure the worth, the value, the meaning, and the quality of your experiences? When it's all over and done, how will you know that you did it as "right" as you could?

How much will you have to change or give up now, today, to have this result and why do that? Are things so bad? Sure, there are momentary lapses when you think there must be more, but what's the harm? Why confuse yourself with this thing called "result?" Things are OK. What's the harm in sticking with the status quo?

No harm. If that's the distance you choose to travel, stick with it. If it keeps you on an even keel, and the disquieting moments have no detrimental waking or sleeping impact on you, read no further. Looking for a new result is not something you should consider or may even need. Satisfy yourself with: "Everyone has moments of doubt." Be content and remember, the reason for this book is to help you enjoy life, not complicate it.

But, what if....

...it's in the "what-if's" that you must find the reason and courage to seek a new final *result*. It's in the "what if is" that you decide to change, to gain, or re-gain the control you relinquished or simply let slip away through neglect. It's in the "what-if's" that we find the holes that need filling. But where to find a strong enough motivation to embark on this journey?

A vision may help.

In your mind's eye, think of the things you want to do but have left undone. Create a clear, colorful, and vivid picture. If you want to sail, smell the salt air, feel the waves, the tiller against your palm. Travel? See the blue sky over the Parthenon, listen for the echo of your step on ancient walks, smell the pine-scented air. Adventure? Hear the rush of wind as you sky-dive toward the green earth, echo with the solid ground as you land and roll on the cool grass. The exhilaration of your own business? Wallow in the satisfaction of saying "I did that!" These are manifestations of your new kind of result. Now, imagine that the pathway to these experiences lies behind a door. Not an ordinary door, a beautifully carved wooden door with golden hinges and a jeweled handle. This door sits isolated, surrounded by an archway, carved of multi-hued Carrara marble. On either side, nothing. A vast emptiness that falls off into inky oblivion. A door standing alone in the cosmos. Your door. The door behind which may be the answer to the result you want for your life.

You approach. All you have to do to have this new adventure is just turn the handle, swing wide the door and walk in. You grasp the cool handle, but you don't open the door. From somewhere deep in the recesses of your mind comes a flood of reasons not to make the move, not to risk a new perspective. These reasons aren't new, you've used them a million times. They make sense. They are part of the mosaic that holds your deceptive world together. Now, are you going to risk disrupting them for a new way of thinking? Yes. Yes, because you've come this far, the door is right there, why turn back? Anyway, you can always reject any new idea. That's your decision.

You open the door. The simplicity of the answer overwhelms you.

> *The result you want is to have lived such a wonderful and extraordinary life that you would delight in living it over again.*

That's it. That's the benchmark one uses to gauge one's life and the relative value of every experience. It's a guideline that helps determine whether to stick with something or move on. A scale to weigh one experience against another. For example, based on as many facts and considerations as I have at my disposal, would I rather repeat this experience or that one? Would I choose to spend one more nano-second with a toxic or restricting person if I knew I would have to spend that time with him or her again, and again? Would I have the guts to bid them a hearty farewell and risk living alone until I find a more uplifting environment? Would I become the attorney my parents want or the artist I want? How would I feel about the regret of being what someone else wanted as opposed to what I wanted? To feel that regret again and again?

Then there are the continual questions one must ask at all times: "How can I fashion a life so filled with life-affirming experiences that the very idea of reliving it makes me giddy? What will I have to do starting right now to be sure I look forward to the next time around, this astounding moment when I took control and made choices that precluded the regret of abdicating my responsibility to me? Remember, you can't go back and change all the life-denying decisions of your past. Even considering that is a waste of time and not the objective. What you can change is how you look at the future and your responsibility to life-affirming activities in that future. Ask yourself. What holds me in thrall? Why do I not follow my bliss? Why would I ever accept a life that I would not choose to re-live?"

Tough questions that form a life, a real life.

Notice that this idea provides no information about any specific experiences you would want to re-live. These choices can be seen only through your lens. Our primary goal, therefore, is to seek what is truly us. No one else can discover the experiences that we will want to repeat.

Also notice there is nothing in this concept about what has passed. It's not important. It's gone, like it or not. Forget it. What are you going to do now? Notice also there is nothing in this concept about which action will prove correct. There are no guarantees. The hard reality is things don't always work out the way we want. What matters, is not whether the experience is perfect or even correct. What matters is that you now have a way of determining the relative value of one course against another. A system for taking personal responsibility for the choices you make, as opposed to being subject to whim, shifting winds, and errant tides that befog our decisions. In short, a compass.

I would love to take credit for this idea. Unfortunately I can't.

It was the philosopher Friedrich Nietzsche who gave the concept its vital life. He called it The Eternal Return or the Eternal Recurrence of the same.

Read very carefully. Re-read very carefully.

> **ETERNAL RETURN**

"What, if some day or night, a demon were to steal after you into your loneliest loneliness and say to you: this life, as you now live it and as you have lived it, you will have to live once more and innumerable times more; and there will be nothing new in it, but every pain and every joy and every thought, every sigh must return to you—all in the same succession and sequence—even this spider and this moonlight between the trees, and even this moment and I myself. The eternal hourglass of existence is turned over again and again—and you with it speck of dust. Would you throw yourself down and gnash your teeth and curse the demon who spoke thus? Or have you once experienced a tremendous moment when you would have answered him: You are a god, and never have I heard anything more divine! If this thought were to gain possession of you, it would change you as you are or perhaps crush you. The question in each and everything, "do you desire this once more and innumerable times more?" would lie upon your actions like the greatest weight. Or how well disposed would you have to become to yourself and to life to crave nothing more fervently than this ultimate eternal confirmation and seal?"

Nietzsche didn't really believe that we, in fact, live our lives over and over again. He wants us to think about how we would live today, and what we would do today if we did. If we really had to live our life over again, and were fully aware of it, what different choices would we make? With each new opportunity or potential experience, we would be keenly aware that if we were afraid, and walked away from opportunity, we would have to relive that inaction time after time. We would always wonder what life might have been like if we had just taken the risk. We would also be keenly conscious of the time we spend in useless, moribund, or dead relationships. Aware of lost time spent in meaningless or demeaning jobs, watching TV, dealing with boring, counterproductive people, hoping things will change, or regretting what is past. Now, we must live with the recurring regret of inaction for all the rest of time.

Stop reading. Spend a few minutes with this idea. Let it take control of you. Try to gain a deep, clear understanding of the Eternal Return. Don't just pass over it as another point in a book that you'll tuck away in a dusty corner. This could mark the time you took charge and found the courage to live the kind of life you want, and not the kind imposed upon you or one for which you settled.

We're also not talking about all those decisions made in the past. All those are gone and you can't fish them out of your memory and experience pond to change them. The Eternal Return question is for this very moment only. The choice you face today, the decision you must make now. Will that choice or decision be one you would make again and live again?

But what if your decision proves the wrong one?

So what? Which decision is ever the "right" decision? There is no way of knowing. It will be what it will be and nothing you can do will change it. But, you can fool the bad decision. How? Love it! Embrace the bad decision, even if it seems the worst decision you could have made. That's a much better choice than wallowing in it and bringing yourself down. If you had not made that decision, any other decision could have worked out just as badly. The difference? You took the responsibility this time. You took it upon yourself to live the kind of life you imagined would fulfill you. You made the decision based on inflicting as little collateral harm as possible. And in making that decision you also have to live with the results. Love it! Love it! Love it! Why would you ever choose to do anything else? Fate, nature, the world, the universe, care not a whit whether you choose to go left or right, whether you do or do not like the rain. They don't care if your tooth aches or you have the best flower garden ever. You alone add the dimension of care to these events. Only you can decide if they are good or bad. Only you can decide to wallow in the agony and revel in the joy. Only you can decide to accept everything as part of the process and love it. Choosing anything else holds no promise of a life worth re- living, only a life unlived.

The idea of *result* and Eternal Return is magnified when we really come to grips with the clear notion of our mortality. This moment at the door is the only moment there will ever be to take this ride without regrets. If that is a clear vision and it wraps its hands tightly around your neck, you will never delude yourself with:

.... "next time, yes, next time I'll do it differently."

This is the only time, and the *result* of your life will depend on it.

Chapter 8

The Path

Puskhar. A small Indian town overlooking an evaporating lake in the distant state of Rajasthan. Stairs lead down to the water where holy men cleanse their lives, laundry women wash their clothes. An aquatic meeting of the mundane and the extra mundane in a land of expected contradiction.

A large block stone juts out over the water. A place to sit.

A muffled afternoon chant lifts from a far minaret.

Time to think.

To have a life worth reliving, that's the result I want from my life. It makes sense. It gives form to choice. It provides a system for determining one direction over another. One relationship over another. One slice of chocolate cake over another. It all but eliminates knee-jerk reaction. It places the responsibility where it always is, on me. The difference in understanding this and not understanding this is that now, I'm aware I'm responsible because I'm forced to examine all choices in a brighter light.

Choosing to have a life worth re-living means your experiences must be dramatic and captivating enough to desire them again. We don't simply re-live, we re-live our experiences. Experience is the key. But how is it that interesting, repeatable, life-affirming experiences happen? Why do interesting experiences seem to happen more to some than others? Is there a single word that answers these questions? In fact, can one word be of such sufficient strength that it actually defines what it is to be human? Can it be sufficient enough in itself so a vital, Aesthetic Human Being is willing to die to protect it? I think so.

In choosing to have the dramatic, life-affirming experiences you would relish repeating, you must have *options!*

Options, *that's it.*

If the desired result of your life is to have a life worth reliving, then that means having experiences worth repeating. To have these experiences, you must have the *option* of choosing, exploring and participating in as many different and exciting alternatives as possible.

For some with a clear and personal fundamental project, that thing that gets you up at first light or keeps you up all night, finding options and participating in experiences is a snap. Options and experiences gravitate to them. These people understand what they want and will do anything to engage the passion of their fundamental project. This passion is perhaps the greatest gift a person can give him or herself. In this passion, one finds a host of repeatable experiences that give meaning to the short stay on earth. For the rest of us the reality of a fundamental project is as vaporous as the next TV talk show. Nothing so captivates us that we are willing to stay up all night peeking through a small hole to study the magic of the night sky. Nothing so enthralls us that we breathe the dust of an ancient tomb to unlock the silent message of an antique civilization.

Ask yourself: What is my fundamental project? Do I have one? If I had to construct one, what would it be?

So, if the key to all this is having and exploring options that allow experiences, where's the problem? Can't you just go exploring? Can't you just do it?

Well, yes and no. True, a vast number of familiar options are available to you at all times. You use and re-use them when needed. Others are not part of who you are or how you think. They are uncomfortable and mysterious. Some are so distant they may not even be within your visible spectrum of possibilities. "Deviant" options, though perhaps a huge part of your fantasy life, are carefully kept at a distance because of unquestioned dogmas, unexamined rules, social protocol, or a map-maker's restrictive influence. Christianity and Islam, as examples, have built and sustained themselves on the premise of prohibition, punishment, and resentment. For one to be a "good Christian" one or a "good Muslim" must restrict a vast array of life-affirming experiences.

The answer then is that you can explore the options you have allowed in, and, if you choose, expand your choice of options. There's the problem. Choosing. It's important first to remember that you are the sum total of the options you have chosen so far. It's also important to know that you become the options you choose, and execute in the future. It's important thirdly that the only chooser is you. No outsider makes the final decision. Fourth, even under the most restrictive conditions, you still have an option. And fifth, even though your choices may be limited by the kind of restrictions your map-maker imposed upon you early in your life, you now have the choice to continue believing these proscriptions or not. This breaking away is one of the most difficult human activities. Remember, you always have an option.

As politically incorrect as it may sound, you always have the option of suicide. I recall the story of a man who, as he grew older, kept his old military 45 by his bed. If he ever felt he could no longer have meaningful life experiences, he had an out. He had no intention of spending his final years hooked up to wires and tubes. One day he was walking in his garden and had a stroke. They took him away in a blaze of flashing red lights to the hospital where they hooked him up to wires and tubes. For more than eighteen months he was subjected to every form of Frankensteinian "life prolonging miracle." For more than eighteen months he was unable to make himself understood. He couldn't control his body in any way. He was at the mercy of others. He had no conscious experiences. It was not what he wanted. He lost his final option. He lost them all.

"Die proudly if it is no longer possible to live proudly." Never lose your option. It is your option no matter what "they" tell you. Although the notion of suicide may seem disturbing, with a little thought, it has the strange power to provide a great deal of comfort. After all, if there is always one option, there must be others. This knowledge also forces upon you an obligation to make the most of each and every day. If you chose not to end it then you have, by default, chosen to live it. In that choice resides the responsibility to do so the best way you can.

Knowing that there is one door frees your creativity to look for others. You are never limited in your options. You are only limited in the way you perceive your selections. Never let anyone tell you that you have no option. Close your eyes and envision a vast field of flowers through which you can run. You have just executed one kind of option. There are more. Look for them.

Let's examine a couple of words that will prove important in understanding options and experiences. It's the idea of necessary and sufficient conditions. Don't let the terms necessary and sufficient conditions confuse you. The concept is fascinating, and an understanding of these terms will prove vastly helpful in how you view and analyze many situations in life.

As we have discussed, the desired result of your life is a life worth reliving. If we then agree that it's vital to have life-affirming experiences to accomplish this result, these kinds of experiences are sufficient, in themselves to assure the result you seek. You need nothing more than these experiences. Anything less would not fill the bill.

To have these kinds of experiences, you need to have options open to you. But an option alone is not sufficient to allow these experiences. Why? Because options have two parts, both of which are necessary. The first necessary condition: the raw availability of the option. This can be real or imagined.

Example: A job you want is open at ABC Company, you can apply for it. This raw availability of the position is a necessary condition for the option of working at ABC. Alone, however, the availability of the option is not sufficient. Enter the second aspect. You must take steps to turn the option into a reality.... filling out the application, sending it in, securing the interview, and following up.

This second aspect too is a necessary, but not in itself a sufficient condition for something to really be an option. If no position is available, you can send in applications all day long and nothing will happen.

An extreme example: You have the imagined option, necessary, of jumping rope on Pluto. You see it clearly in your mind and fantasize on it day and night Problem is you have no way of getting to Pluto, also necessary if you are going to turn the option into an experience. A sufficient condition for jumping rope on Pluto therefore, is contingent on speculating about jumping rope *and* taking the action to bring it to life. In this example, almost nothing you can do will bring the experience to life, so it will never really happen. You will never reach the sufficient conditions. You can of course, start building a rocket ship that will take you and your jump rope to Pluto and call my bluff (one should always have unattainable and fanciful ideas), but most people would say you won't be successful. So what! If you enjoy the idea, it harms no one, and it gives you pleasure, go for it. That may well be the kind of experience you desire to repeat time and time again.

Let's look at this process as an A, B, C.

- A. Life-affirming, repeatable experiences are sufficient to constitute having a life worth reliving.
- B. Having and executing a wide range of different and new and personally important options are sufficient to create life-affirming experiences.
- C. 1. Access, real or imagined, to an option is necessary to having life-affirming experiences.
     2. Execution of options is necessary to having life-affirming experiences.

We are once again talking about personal responsibility. If you are going to have experiences, it's not enough just to read about them, you have to *do* them. If you read about SCUBA diving but never get wet, you may not find the experience exhilarating enough to want to repeat it. How many times do you want to watch a re-run of a TV program?

Here's the big difference between imagining and doing.

The human animal fantasizes about the necessary conditions for options to take shape. He reads the books or takes the course. He may pile necessary condition upon necessary condition in hopes of deluding himself into believing that he is having a true experience. In short, he keeps options and experience at a distance in hopes of being safe.

The Aesthetic Human Being starts with the first necessary condition of speculation then adds the second necessary condition of action. Only there does one find experiences worth living and reliving.

A simple question.

Which are you?

⌛

Chapter 9

Necessary Conditions

Options don't just appear. Options require further ground or the conditions for the possibility of becoming visible, being manipulated, accepted, or rejected. If you don't expect unexpected things to happen, they won't. They'll hide. The more you create the conditions for unique possibility, the more likely it is that exciting new options will creep out of dark corners and captivate you, send you into a new arena. You have to be open. Think of it this way. You are in a vast parking lot, looking for your car. At this point, your world is two things: you, looking for your car, and your car. Everything else mainly falls out of your field of vision. You're not really open to anything else until you find your car. At this moment, you have limited the possibility of something else capturing your attention. You have reduced your options.

A sad truth: many people spend their entire lives "looking for their car" and missing most of the things around them.

Now for the really big question. The one whose answer can let you look for your car and also be open to new options. Can you improve the soil, the conditions for the possibility of endless options? Are there fundamental components of options that can be manipulated and influenced to improve the conditions for the possibility of even more options and even more life-affirming experiences?

There are six.

Each of the six is necessary to help create more options. None alone is sufficient, or has enough power alone to do so.... Water is a necessary requirement for a human life, but by itself it is not sufficient to keep one alive.

If you are going to establish the conditions for the possibility of more options you'll need these components:

1. Health
2. Freedom
3. Knowledge
4. Motivation
5. Courage
6. Wealth

As the combination of gas, air, and spark is sufficient to run an engine, the combination of these six components is sufficient for creating all the options you need. The only question is, will you breathe life into each element?

I have given these components a ranking, from health at one, to wealth at six. You may not agree with this ranking, but one must start somewhere. You also may not agree that the six cover every possibility. Add your own. I have included many important concepts under these six that may indeed be independent. Friends, for example, could be an independent component. I have chosen to include it under Health. A healthy person has a support system that includes friends. To keep things as simple as possible, try to fit one of your personal components within one of the six. It will force you to think a bit more about how the puzzle fits together. The ranking is also not set in stone. It changes as situations change. I have ranked them based on how the lack of them would affect the average person. Don't get hung up on my ranking. Be flexible and interpret as needed. Go for understanding.

In addition to the personal aspect of the six components, there is a business side. For a business to grow, it too needs all six components. A growing business needs motivation, it needs courage, it needs wealth, etc. If you want to take a side trip, think about your business from these points of view. It will prove very profitable.

⧗

Chapter 10

Health

Without reservation, I place being healthy as the most important requirement for opening new options. A deeply ill person is almost incapable of focusing on anything outside himself and his illness... a creature in pain is more pain than creature. It's incidental whether he has the knowledge to explore new options. Incidental whether he is motivated. Incidental whether he is free. His focus is on the illness, and everything else is obscured by dark clouds. Of course, if you're just a little sick, you may indeed place wealth at the top of your list. Without money, you don't have the option of going to the doctor.

Health is divided into two parts, physical and mental. Although they are interdependent, I will treat them separately.

Physical health

For the purposes of this book, I define physical health as the actual physical ability to have a "full range" of experience without being restricted by pain or mechanical devices. An example. Not long ago I had to give a talk in London. Two days before I was to leave I tripped and really hurt my foot. The x-ray showed nothing, but the swelling and the pain remained. When I got to London, I was unable to do much walking at all. I gave my presentation sitting on a stool as opposed to walking around the audience as I always do. I also wanted badly to see all the sights of London, but because I was "unhealthy" I didn't have the option of touring around on foot the way I hoped. My physical health closed that option. Granted, my pain didn't prevent me from taking a cab or a bus, but it did limit many other options like walking around museums. In this case, I was able to use a bit of creativity to get around and the pain didn't keep me in the hotel. But suppose I had actually broken the foot? First, I would have not gone to London, and second, I might have been in such pain that I couldn't even think of creative ways of accommodating the injury. I would have focused strictly on the pain, and the experience of London would have had no importance.

Another example, a person needing dialysis every few days would not opt for a long trip down the Congo River. There may be no medical facilities for hundreds of miles much less a dialysis machine. Her options are limited.

The physically healthy person can have a "full range" of experiences without being restricted. Notice that I have placed "full range" in quotes. A person needing dialysis is still fully capable of unique and life-affirming experiences of all sorts. They may just be a bit more limited. Unless one is dead or unconscious, there is always a vast array of life-affirming experiences available. Often with physical ill health, assuming it is not completely incapacitating, the first few weeks or months restrict options the most. During this time the person focuses only on the problem and most options vanish. In time, the person starts to find new creative ways to adapt to the conditions, often turning it into an exciting adventure. This physical ill health has changed only the context of their lives, not the responsibility. Our responsibility is not to complain and rail about our circumstances and limitations. Our responsibility is to shape, carve and manipulate those circumstances and limitations into all sorts of experiences that achieve our own special result. This is where we make use of our best creativity.

A metaphor: If you are suddenly made of wood, your physical make-up should discourage you from running into a burning house. If you are made of wood and want more than anything in your life to run into a burning house, you should do so and accept the consequences. If you are made of wood and want to run into a burning house, but you still want to have life-affirming experiences, you must make yourself incombustible, then run into the burning house.

Challenge, creativity, activity. Three most delicious words.

Physical health is so critical to options that you must develop a driving passion to gain or maintain it. The decision should never be whether to smoke or not. It should be whether to quit now or in five seconds. It should never be whether to exercise or not, it should be, "which gym can I join today?" The responsibility for your physical health rests on no one but you. The people who write about health only report. They do nothing about what's on your plate. The cook at the "all the fried chicken you can eat for $1.00" doesn't care if you are already eighty pounds overweight or have diabetes. It's not his job. The care for all this is yours and trying to blame it on the negligent health-care system or the lure of TV advertising is the highest form of self-neglect and self-deception. You and you alone are responsible and you and you alone will suffer, not the smiling gal flipping burgers or the TV announcer hawking a giant gooey milkshake.

To have options that lead to life-affirming, repeatable experiences, take care of your physical health. Ask yourself, whether a given behavior is likely to lead to something debilitating. If it is, stop doing it.

A friend of mine is a painter and a model maker. He does wonders with his hands. He also loves to ride mountain bikes. Not long ago he took a header down a hill and banged himself up badly. My question to him was simple: could riding your mountain bike greatly injure your hands? Yes, no doubt it could. Would a hand injury limit many other options you think important, i.e., painting? Yes. Are you willing to risk this loss? No. His challenge then is to find a way to enjoy his mountain bike and protect his hands.

During my college years I piloted a plane for a crazy bunch of sky-divers. They always wanted me to learn to jump, even offering to teach me free. I thought long and hard about it, weighing the relative value of jumping with the potential problems associated with a bad landing or dropping dead at 12,000 feet. In the end, I determined the relative value of sky-diving was not worth the risk of potentially not being able to do other things I felt more important. I didn't feel I was copping out, just valuing the potential loss to the potential gain.

One rule for maintaining your physical health: try never to do anything that might preclude you from doing other things that you deem more important. Smoke and you won't be healthy enough to climb steps, much less a mountain. My dad died of emphysema after smoking for half a century. His last days were spent in a wheelchair connected to an oxygen tank. With no stretch of the imagination anyone can see his range of options was greatly limited. His unhealthy choice closed other options.

There is one caveat: be sure you aren't playing games with yourself and making excuses or rationalizing inaction.

If you are already on the road to physical ill health, get help and take charge. If you are beyond help, enjoy the ride as best you can. Find the most creative and enjoyable ways to get along. The choice of enjoying even this last flight into the unknown is a choice you should work to make relivable.

The final act is no different than all the other acts of your life. They too will evaporate and leave not a rack behind. Give this final part of the parade its untarnished worth. Enjoy it all.

Mental health

The second kind of health is mental health.

Mental health is the ability to recognize and understand that an alternative is even possible at all.

A mentally unhealthy person is bounded by her world, context bound, and will defend this limited world view to all attacks. She will do the same thing again and again, unable to realize there are other choices. She will be unwilling even to explore whether this choice is or is not working for her. She is not interested in options, seeing them as scary, deviant, and undermining. This closed context is important in helping maintain her world and keeping it on an even keel. Trying to change her is difficult, if not impossible. Suggesting change or alternatives often leads to irreconcilable hostility.

Change is not her wish, within her vista or maybe even within her realm of possibility. Here, the option door is closed, and opening it requires help beyond the ability of most.

The mentally healthy person on the other hand, is keenly aware that new options and new experiences demand a change in context. He is willing to suspend his view of his existing context, allowing in new ideas. He will embrace different points of view and weigh them against what he knows, or suspects, but not against what he "knows is right." He will work diligently to hold personal prejudices at bay until the worth of an alternative has been fully explored. He will admittedly defend his belief, but will gladly yield to the power of a better argument. He is a fallibilist. (Fallibism: the doctrine that no statement can be accepted as true beyond all possible doubt.)

A mentally healthy person knows the difference between "I can't" and "I won't." If an "offensive" or suspect book is presented to the "I can't" person, they will turn their head in coy embarrassment, pretending it is just too much for them to take. Far too often that "I can't" (as opposed to something impossible, i.e., I can't be 25 again)" is dubious and steeped in external restrictions. It is also the result of chazzing" ("Chazzing." Holding a deep and vocal opinion on a subject about which you have no knowledge or experience whatsoever.) Like so many things in their lives, that suspect book is just one more thing that they have eliminated without thinking.

"I won't" is what I call the existential negation. It implies that the person has at least thought about something and has, based on his or her experience, decided not to read that book or take that action. As with almost everything in this book, the "I won't" negation is the only one that has any merit. It means the person has taken responsibility for what they will or won't do and is not ducking that responsibility without thought, study or actual experience.

Never confuse the two. You are only fooling yourself.

Another barometer of good mental health is demonstrated by how easily you are offended. As a rule if you are mentally healthy, you don't take things so personally that you give them the power to offend. Once offended, you have relinquished control of your emotions to something outside yourself. The offender got you. He found your hot button and manipulated you. Not something you want.

Also, offense, at its core, is your problem. Somewhere along the way you learned that a given statement or action is offensive …in the eye of the beholder as it were. Nothing is offensive in and of itself. There is no Platonic "form" of the offensive. Like most things in life, value is determined by you.

To explore this notion, contrast offense and confusion. Almost by definition, offense is a monologue and confusion a dialogue. Someone offends you, you respond with a defense or a jump to a moral high-ground. "How could you say that? You're just a bigot! I refuse to talk about that!" The result is two people having monologues about their opinions. Nothing is accomplished.

What if instead of responding with a defense, you responded with questions? This would initiate a dialogue and eliminate the hostility generally associated with offense. You might also learn something about the situation or the other person you didn't know.

The first questions should be to yourself: How did I learn to be offended by this statement or action? Exactly what about this offends me? Is my offense justified or just knee-jerk? Does this person know he is offending me? (There are two kinds of offense, one of intent and one of ignorance. Be sure you know the difference.) Why would I allow this person this kind of control over me? These internal questions force you to pause and reflect.

The next questions can be directed toward the offender: Where did you get this opinion? Are there places where this kind of opinion is okay? Is there something in your life that caused you to think this way?

Spinoza, a philosopher who was kicked out of religions and countries, had a great way of looking at this. When faced with an "offensive" person, he would say to them: "if I had been brought up the way you were, had the experiences you had, and thought like you did, I would feel the same way about this situation as you." This simple statement precluded judgment and kept Spinoza on an even keel.

Offense is a monologue. Confusion is a dialogue. The latter

is one manifestation of mental health. The former, the opposite.

A mentally unhealthy person also does not have the ability to recognize his actual limitations and weaknesses. This is, of course, a slippery slope. Should any of us seeking new experiences admit to or accept limits or weaknesses? Yes, but only when proceeding in a given direction is either patently absurd or disastrous, "I can breathe, unassisted, underwater," or, "I can actually make love on one of the moons of Jupiter."

But it's in challenging and overcoming our limitations and weaknesses that we find vast, unplowed fields of growth, new options and life-affirming experiences. Therefore, limitations are a question of recognition and action. If I don't understand that I can't fly, unaided, and should not jump off the building, then I am unhealthy. If I want to fly and recognize that without aid, I will fall, I'm healthy. The healthy person will understand his or her limitations, embrace them, and find creative ways to overcome or get around them.

⏳

Chapter 11

Freedom

I can think of no more daunting task than discussing freedom. Its true nature and requirements are understood by no one. Still, I proceed.

Assuming you are healthy, freedom is the central hub around which all of your other options rotate. If you are not free, you will never be able to expand your options. Granted, there have been times when the loss of freedom caused some of the most heroic and exciting experiences in the history of mankind. Ask any resistance fighter about those moment in his life, and you will notice high excitement when he tells you about taking the train or blowing up the bridge. This kind of activity is exhilarating and may indeed be the central issue or event in someone's life.

I knew a man who fought in World War II in the Pacific. As a young Marine he was in the first wave of men who landed on three different islands. He was wounded twice and almost died in a sandy fox hole. Before he died a couple of years ago the only topic of conversation that would animate him was about the war. With each conversation, I had the distinct feeling that everything after that was just so much noise and an anticlimactic blur surrounding the rest of his life. When pressed, he would tell me how awful it was and how he lost so many buddies. But in the same breath he would go on to explain in detail how enticing and exhilarating it was to be in those situations. I never asked him if he would choose to re-live that time. I suspect if I had, he would have said no, not on your life. Asked if he would choose not to have had the experience, he would also have answered no. As I think back to what he told me of his life, and the way he was in those last years, I think his involvement in WW II may well have been the single most important event in his whole life. His fight for freedom was an experience beyond anything else.

But as I was saying, the radical loss or absence of freedom closes options, and the loss of options must be fought at all costs.

But what kind of freedom? Freedom within limits. There's no other kind. No one is ever truly free. We're all limited in some way. Freedom, therefore, is always a fight to overcome things in one's self and in one's time that limit the options you wish to have. This fight is conducted on two levels. The first level is internal, a fight against the restrictions imposed by yourself, on yourself. These are the hardest kind because they are so difficult to see. The second level is external, a fight against restrictions imposed from the outside. In both cases, one should always be aware of these restrictions and strive to overcome them, finding options and therefore new experiences.

When external freedom is absolutely limited and there is truly nothing you can do, you should accept immediate limitations with as much grace as possible and try to find creative distractions and projects. It smoothes the way to accepting these limitations. Under no circumstances however should you ever fully resign your self to limitations. Full resignation is just a small step from the channel changer.

To add depth to the notion of freedom, I'll divide freedom into three different kinds. Each of these is necessary to the whole of freedom. If one is missing, the vast and dramatic field of options will be a closed door to all comers.

The three types of freedom:
1. Freedom from
2. Freedom to
3. Freedom can

1. Freedom From
Freedom From is the expected kind of freedom: Freedom From repression. The kind of repression found under a totalitarian ruler,

boss, fascist government, or tyrannical religion. It's in totalitarianism that the members of a society are radically limited in thoughts and actions. A repressive society demands conformity and adherence to strict rules of conduct, random laws, and moral edicts without election or choice. Transgressions are avoided for fear of personal or spiritual retribution. In this kind of society, options fail to grow. Relivable experiences are few and far between.

An overtly totalitarian society is easy to see. Easy to feel its iron hand around your neck. It has a police force with harsh forms of punishment. Given the idea that freedom means overcoming restrictions in one's time, the fight against these kinds of regimes has provided some of man's most worthwhile challenges. These fights have also provided some of man's most exciting and repeatable experiences. Think of the day the Berlin wall fell. Those there will remember that day and would likely relish the opportunity to repeat it. When a society accepts fascist rulers and allows options to be smothered with fear of retribution, life-affirming experiences vanish. When rebellion and revolution blossom, life-affirming experiences thrive.

When a society fails to open doors to new thinking or when it censors thought and actions, it is doomed to tumble under the creative attacks of those with more options and more ways to circumvent harsh restrictions. Without exception, the more options you have, the greater the chance you will out-maneuver everyone else. The more options you have, the less the chance your opponent will be able to guess your next move. The more options you have, the more you will ultimately control your situation.

In the long run, options will win.

There is another kind of repressive society, more insidious, more restrictive, and damaging: the moral society. In the moral society, select groups determine correct and incorrect behavior and beliefs. In a moral society, unique interpretations and new ideas are avoided, shunned, or precluded to protect the current tyrannical reign of morality. In this tyrannical, moral society the power of the phrase "thou shalt not" yields fertile ground to nurture human bigots and wrathful gods. Excessive morality can breed a society of inquisition, ethnic cleansing, eternal damnation and banishment, Northern Ireland/Afghanistan. In a moral society, the acquisition of certain kinds of knowledge is considered an absolute evil and prohibited from the very start of human existence. Evil and prohibited for no reason. No justification. Through morality, resentment and political correctness become rule and law. It's in the moral society that the majestic and awe-inspiring notion of ethics and personal responsibility are eclipsed by papistry, ecclesiastical paternalism and standards of behavior rooted in aristocratic, self-serving antiquity. It's morality that randomly lifts words from a single source and turns them into hate, extortion, and prohibition. These abstruse words are interpreted and reinterpreted by those with enough power and influence to force standards of behavior. It's through morality that the ethical responsibility to do no physical harm to another turns into witch-burning and crusades. It's through morality, that rationality is overcast with moral dogma that passes judgment and prevents people from living a life worth re-living. It is in the moral society where dominion over the other creatures results in the loss of species after species without regard for the ethics of stewardship.

In a society dominated by bigoted little people, one is not free to ask the questions, questions to enlighten and expand the scope of knowledge, the scope of options, the scope of experience. It is indeed a hideous restriction of freedom if an individual believes that he is guilty by conception, guilty without trial or jury for something in which he had no part but for which he must constantly redeem himself. At that point one's options, if one believes such superstition and mythology, must be limited to finding impossible ways to absolve oneself of this randomly-placed condemnation. To further limit one's options, one is extorted into believing that all experience today is valueless and that all effort must be directed toward a vaporous afterlife, an afterlife promised only through translation, resentment, hyperbole, and the resentful times that give it literary form and social weight. To sacrifice known, life-affirming experiences of today for a make-believe after-life is the highest form of self-deception. What is the point of an afterlife except to denigrate and demean this life? Any social structure demanding that a set of contradictory doctrines be viewed as the answer to man's quest for meaning is a farce and should be relegated to the dustbin of history.

Guard your ethics, they are yours. Morality will be determined and imposed by others. Don't listen. You know what's right, don't you?

In addition to Freedom From restrictive tyrants, governments, and religion, you must also find a Freedom From the domination and opinions of a host of other people. At some magical or dramatic point, you must decide that the restrictions placed on you by your history are just that, history. You must also learn that the responsibility of free choice can no longer be passed off to someone else. This Freedom From is the path to a whole new set of options. When we sift through all the "facts" and "morals" that have been drilled into us, we can decide if they are life-stultifying or life-affirming. Through editing our internal boundaries we can appreciate other people as they pass through the revolving door of our life. Some of them we want to stay. We learn from them. The others, the toxic ones, we let revolve out. From them, we learn only what we don't want to learn again.

Life is far too short. Leave the toxic ones in and life will seem far too long. Abandon the essential you and your road has no vanishing point, only a diurnal flatness and vexation.

2. Freedom To

Of the three freedoms, the Freedom To is the most important. It is the freedom over which you have the most control. The fight for true individual freedom is always a fight to overcome things inside yourself that limit your options.

How is Freedom To different from Freedom From? Freedom From requires an outside agent. The tyrant. The repressor. Freedom To is the freedom you have within yourself. Freedom To involves the radical and all-encompassing responsibility you have to yourself to have a full range of life-affirming experiences, with no excuses for not doing so. Every door must be opened no matter how difficult it may seem to do so. Here is where you come face to face with all the bogus reasons for not taking advantage of as many new possibilities as you can. Being Free To means not lying to yourself.

In simple terms, Freedom To means you are always personally responsible for what you choose and for what you don't chose. You are even responsible for choices that you have excluded from your field of exploration. These options must be included if you are to determine accurately the full range of possibilities. Only by rejecting excuses can you expand options and enhance your experiences. If you are afraid of starting your own business because your dad tried and failed, you have limited your thinking through history. Because your father failed, there is no reason to believe you will. That understanding is a critical part of Freedom To. History in itself is interesting but useless in a life actively seeking experience. If you fall back on past failures or successes and proceed no further, history becomes an anchor. Not a learning process. Not a guide.

In the true concept of Freedom To, an excuse for not taking or considering any action is unacceptable. There are no excuses. There is only "I have reviewed as many options as I could and considering everything, I choose not to take this action."

Again, there is never a time when you are without choice.

There is another kind of Freedom To summed up in one word: fearlessness. Fear comes when you feel you can't defend yourself from many of the "controllable" vicissitudes of life. There are a vast array of things you can't control. We can't control the thousand natural shocks to our health, but we can have insurance. A rumbling earthquake will level your office in a matter of seconds. A tornado will turn a mobile home into twisted steel under a dark cloud. These things are beyond your control. You can, however, control how you prepare for and react to events. A "safe" place in your office during an earthquake, or an underground hiding place in a tornado are excellent "controls." Fresh water, food, and a flashlight in expectation of uncontrollable events are insurance and integral to enhancing fearlessness.

You fear when you carry excessive debt, then can't defend yourself from economic adversity. When you buy gas-thirsty, hulking cars, then fear scarcity. When you eat excessively, then fear for your health. When you stop learning, then become confused and immobilized at the unfolding of alien events. When you act responsibly you educate yourself in a broad range of subjects. Fearlessness then prevails and you are Free To open yourself to a wider range of possibilities and experiments. You no longer fear the things you don't understand. Demons are declawed by learning about them.

Find something you fear. Study that fear. Learn about it. Take an action toward the fear, then overcome it. The overcoming of your fears may be the most interesting adventure of your life.

You can choose to do that.

3. Freedom Can

This final freedom is the least complicated. Even if you are free in every other respect to do something, are the conditions such that you can actually do it? The critical difference between Freedom From, Freedom To and Freedom Can is simple ability. You're totally free to join a health club, there's no law or prohibition against it... Freedom From. You've run out of personal excuses not to... Freedom To. Problem now is you may live in a town with no health club, so there is nothing to join... Freedom Can.

To take it a step further. There is a club in town, you join, you go to the bench to pump some iron. Under no known conditions will you ever be able to bench press two thousand pounds. You have the other two freedoms but you don't have this one. The lack of this freedom will preclude your entering a contest for those who can bench press more than fifteen hundred pounds.

In Washington both the rich and the poor are free to sleep on the grates on a cold night. They both can do that. But to sleep in the Hilton . . .

The difficulty in understanding Freedom Can involves how you look at *rationalizations* (excuses) for not executing your freedom, and true *conditions* for not doing so. One person's rationalization is another person's condition. The distinction is tough and always subjective. Excuses are deceitful. They have a cunning way of assuming the pleasing and irresponsible shapes, guises, and forms of conditions.

Try this. Next time you face a new situation where you may be able to exercise your freedom instead of jumping to an habitual negative conclusion, ask the following questions:

1. Do you have the actual ability to exercise the freedom in question? Is there anything at all that would physically preclude you from the activity? Example: Sky diving. Can you get in a parachute? Can you get in the plane? Can you actually jump? Can you fall through the air? Can you land on your feet? If you can do these things then you *can* sky dive. If you wanted to go swimming but had no arms, by definition, you *can not* swim free style. None of these questions ask you if you *want* to, just *can* you.

2. If you can actually execute the freedom, what is the source of your negative attitude toward doing so?

3. What is the credibility of this source?

4. Have you actually experienced the activity in which you now feel you are not free to participate? If so, what happened? If not, you're chazzing. (Holding a deep and vocal opinion on a subject about which you have no knowledge of experience whatsoever.)

5. Do you know someone who has directly participated in this activity?

6. What is the credibility of this source?

7. Have you directly experienced any fallout from anyone who has participated in this activity? For example, have you ever had to take someone to a doctor because they injured themselves skydiving?

8. Does your interpretation of this fallout extend to a universe wider than a single source?

9. Is your source the media?

10. Is the information presented by the media complete?

11. Does the information presented by the media represent a statistical base allowing for a decision relative to a broad spectrum or is it just one "hot" incident?

12. Do you believe everything the media has to say?

13. Have you really thought about how badly you want to take this action?
14. Is not taking this action something you would regret having missed?
15. What is the downside risk of taking this action?
16. How likely is this downside?

Pausing to consider the answers allows you time to either take the action or know why not. If you really know why you are choosing to or not to do something, you are making a conscious choice and that's what a responsible person is all about.

A guiding direction: if a debate is taking place within yourself, assume you are working on a rationalization or an excuse. When a real precluding condition exists, there is little argument.

Also watch for others letting you get away with excuses. When I was just under two, I had polio. I was saddled with braces and crutches for a couple of years. Getting around presented some challenges. My mother tells a story of a day at the swimming pool. She was sitting with a bunch of friends and I was coming over to see her. About fifteen feet away I fell. Crutches, braces, legs and feet went in all directions. "Come on, get up," she said as I struggled to get up. At that point all of her friends "came to my rescue" and chided her about being so unfeeling and making me struggle up on my own. She looked at them and back at me. "Come on, get up." Ignoring her friends was perhaps the best thing that could ever have happened to me.

Dear Mother, did I ever thank you for your courage in not letting me get away with not stretching to the full limit?

Keep an eye on other people when they use excuses for inaction. They'll drag you into their web and your pity will be of no help. If there is a true precluding condition, though, give everything you've got.

The exciting aspect of the third freedom is that one can always work toward an ability to do something. Often a "can" or "cannot" restriction is limited to the imagination one brings to the situation. If you can't bench press two thousand pounds given the rules of the game, change the rules. If the rules don't state that you can't use a crane, use a crane. Let the officials yell and scream. For the creative mind, overcoming the limitations is an exciting challenge. For the lazy and the accepting mind, it's an excuse for inertia. Which are you? Remember, freedom is having the strength to be responsible to oneself. How elegant.

Chapter 12
Knowledge

Defining knowledge is no easy task. The entire field of epistemology is dedicated to understanding how we know and the limits of that knowledge. We must start somewhere.

Knowledge, a starting definition.

The acquaintance with and understanding of sufficient facts, truths, or principles to allow you to recognize, execute, improve, and expand your options.

Simply, the more you know, the more options you will have from which to choose. Limit your study, limit your options.

There are two kinds of knowledge. The first, empirical. Knowledge through direct participation. Here we learn the real lessons of life and find the actual worth of experiences. The overwhelming experiences that we want to remember and repeat, or not repeat, come from the knowledge gained from direct participation. By thrusting our senses into the hot and cold, light and dark, soft and hard of the world, the more we learn and the more we reinforce our desire to find similar experiences. Also, the more we increase our knowledge based on experience, the more doors we open to an even wider range of possibilities. The more attuned our senses become to the variety of stimulation and sensual activities available, the more we will work on building a storehouse of options that encourage repeatable experiences.

Knowledge engenders options. Options spawn experiences. Experience enlarges knowledge.

New knowledge creates new contexts. New contexts create new options.

Acts reinforce action. The circle of experience closes.

It's also by directly partaking of the world that we collide with other people and their experiences. It's here that we can grow or be limited. It's here that new knowledge is either introduced or forbidden. Under no circumstances should you let anyone limit your experiences without your permission or without a full understanding of their reasons. Being warned not to touch a hot stove is excellent knowledge, not an attempt to limit your experience. You can still touch the stove if you wish, and should do so if it is the best or only way you can learn. The consequences will be yours.

"Don't eat of the tree of knowledge." "If you want slaves then you are a fool to educate them as masters." It's your responsibility to learn, to go out into your world and taste, smell, feel, listen, and touch everything. Nothing should stop you. Let sand and long brown hair run through your fingers with sensual delight. Listen to the sea and watch the gliding birds. Travel and learn the ways of others. Swim in the seas of the world and your own world will grow far wider than the edges of where you now stand.

The second type of knowledge is through study, the academic kind, the kind we get from books and classes. Study often lays the foundation for activity, but not always. It is not unusual to find someone burying his head in a book, reading about adventure while the world of adventure goes on all about him. Academic knowledge is benign and will increase your understanding of things to do, things not to do. Burning or banning a book is an action designed only to limit your experience and prevent you from entering arenas where others want to hold all the cards. When Hitler moved into parts of the Soviet Union, the first thing he did was eliminate education for that population. He frequently burned books. Why? Knowledge evokes questions. Answers open doors. Knowledge expands horizons. Why would anyone ever want to keep a people stupid? Interesting question, isn't it? Remember, if someone else knows something and you don't, they have more options. They have the advantage. Read everything. Let nothing stop you.

The pitfall of study: studying, not doing. This doesn't mean that the academic world is not important for opening options. It is. Between ink-marked pages, new and distant ideas and possibilities are born. It's here that knowledge and understanding of what's already out there becomes available for interpretation, re-interpretation, and application. Here is the grounding for more learning, but this alone is not enough. I recall far too clearly a book I read about sex. I was about fifteen. The book was clear, concise, very informative, and very sexy. When the actual time came to put that knowledge to use, the charts, delicious anatomical drawings, and statements about where things were, what they did, and what to do with them were as useless as ancient Egyptian Hieroglyphics. Nothing was where they said it would be, and nothing proceeded as clearly and cleanly as in the book. They failed to mention the effect of passion on understanding and recall. I had the theory but it lacked the skill that comes only with hands-on experience. My brother-in-law once asked my sister if she had ever read a book about someone reading a book. She paused.

For academic knowledge to be of any use in finding options, it must work in concert with action. At some point you must put aside the academic learning and go for the real thing. You can't learn about sex sitting on the side of the bed.

Get in! Get wet. Get wet with a passion. Do everything with a passion. Why not?

I was in Vancouver giving a talk. It was a cool rainy day. Late in the afternoon, after my talk, I went to Chinatown to walk around and experience the afternoon turning into evening. There was a large spice store on a street corner. It was open to the cool and the rain. I stood under an awning watching the people, listening to the dripping rain. I was standing between two big tubs of cloves. I put my hand on top of the cloves and closed my eyes. The sound of the people walking, the rain and the feel of the cloves took over. I took a deep breath and the aroma of spices mixed with the humid air swirled in my head. Another breath and I could pick out a slight perfume of a someone passing by. I stood there for a long while letting all my senses have their way with me.

The knowledge I gained from that spicy, humid street in Vancouver lingers in my mind and with my cells as potently as any knowledge I have in all my life.

Living means being aware. Really living means really being aware. Really being aware means really living. The two are you. You are the two.

Be aware. It's the father of knowledge. Use your knowledge. It's the mother of living.

Chapter 13
Motivation

As already stated, options don't just appear. Finding them means going out and diggin' 'em up, or opening your mind and letting them in. It doesn't mean waiting and hoping they'll just come along. They won't. It takes motivation. It takes action.

What is motivation, and how does it relate to its twin, passion?

Motivation exists only in action. Four ingredients are required for motivation to rear its head.

First, a clear and understandable goal. No one has ever just been motivated. Don't believe me? Try it, get motivated. Not about anything, just motivated. You can't. The clearer your vision of what you want, the more life you give it, the more you focus on it, the more the motivation grows. A worthy goal demands specificity. Exactly how many cars do you want? Exactly when will you finish learning French? By what criteria will you determine when your project is finished? What three things will be different when your project is completed? Be specific with both the quality and the quantity of your objective. Motivation demands clarity, and if you want more options and experiences, you'll need to know exactly what you must do to get them.

Second, commit to the goal. If you can't buy into the goal at a gut level, it will have no vitality and you will give it only a cursory effort. Commit to time frame. If your goal takes more than a year and a half to achieve, find a way to renew it after about fifteen months. It's almost impossible to sustain a strong commitment without renewal. That goes for almost everything in your life. One way to achieve this is to set benchmarks along the way. Achieving these benchmarks will spur you on towards achieving the larger goal.

When I was a kid my sister and I wanted a TV. My dad told us if we saved a percentage of the cost he would kick in the rest. We knew how much we needed to make a TV a reality, so we set a target date for getting it. My mother made a cloth sack out of something I remember looking like mattress ticking and we kept it safe in the closet. Each week we would take out the sack and count the loot to see if we had achieved our goal. At the end of the allotted time, we took the sack to our dad, he counted it. Two days later, we had a new Zenith TV. We set our goal, we had benchmarks, we stuck with it and we learned how to eat off TV trays.

If opening your options means working with other people and motivating them, set benchmarks for them too, then celebrate their achievement. Celebration of benchmarks adds fuel to the fire of motivation. Achievement without celebration is like a gift without wrapping. Take time to reward yourself and others along the way. Make each of these rewards as memorable as possible. Remember, the result is always a life worth reliving. Why not try making each experience as worthy as you can?

Third, for motivation to really take hold you must see how your activity is relevant to achieving the overall goal. The more clearly your activities relate to achieving the goal, the more motivated you will be. If what you are doing has little relevance to the goal, you will bring no passion to the activity, or even quit. A completely clear goal tells you not only what to do but what not to do. Don't let useless activities hamper your achieving what you want. I find when I sit down to write, my refrigerator needs cleaning. A noble activity, but useless in writing a book. Again, if your goal of finding more options requires working with other people, show them how what they are doing relates to the whole. Be specific and be sure they know how integral their effort is to making things happen. The effort they will put forth will astound everyone concerned. People are delighted, if not compelled, to contribute if the goal is clear and they can see how their efforts close the circle.

As I write this chapter, we are one day past the terrorist attack on the World Trade Center and the Pentagon. Yesterday, September 11, 2001 is one of those days that will always remain a clear window into our collective memory; the two planes crashing into the WTC buildings, a third into the Pentagon, one down in Pennsylvania, and the fire as it engulfed the top floors. Then, these two monuments to man's engineering ability tumbling to the earth in a homicidal white puff that ended so many lives.

I watched the news for most of the day. Firemen, police, EMT's, city workers and average citizens jumped into the confusing inferno. Dust and debris made any effort arduous if not perilous. As I sat there in the comfort of my home I considered the motivations of the people entering the fray. I always believe that people do things for one and only one reason, because there is something in it for them. I still believe this. So, I questioned, what's in it for an ordinary citizen? Why risk so much? I tossed and turned last night trying to settle the events of the day and also come to grips with the motivation … the self-motivation that drives people to make such a sacrifice.

My first answer was the easy one. Perhaps their efforts would be found out by CNN and they would be deemed a hero. Yes, for some that may be a motivation. Their fifteen minutes of fame. But I didn't really think that was the overarching reason.

My second argument made a bit more sense. There was a clear goal: "People in there need my help." Clear action: "I can go in, get them and bring them out." The two elements of motivation had been satisfied, a clear goal and a belief that your action would help achieve that goal. I was not satisfied. Even if motivated, why risk everything? Perhaps, I thought, we, as Americans, are compelled to be of assistance or we will feel less about who we are in this society. It's in our collective blood from the very start. It is one of the special things that works so well to hold this diverse country together. Also, I know if I were in the rubble, I would want someone to come help me and if I don't do it now, someone else may not if I need it. That makes it important to me. Motivation has only one face: what's in it for me. Motivation takes many forms: I feel better about myself if I help. I feel better about myself if I take care of my kids. I feel better about myself if I finish my education.

As I listened to the TV interviewer talk to the cops and firemen, I couldn't help feeling that the self-sacrifice was indeed two-fold—the actual reactive training, and the peer pressure that attends being a part of that group. If they fail, the whole team fails and they "couldn't live with themselves."

What's to be learned? To motivate people, have that clear goal. "We need blood." Show them how their actions help achieve this goal. "You can give blood." To sustain the motivation, show them what's in it for them. "How would you feel about yourself if you came to the rescue?" Don't focus strictly on the economic aspect of the reward. That will motivate but not sustain. Look for emotional motivation. "Think how you will feel when, as a doctor, you bring a newborn baby into the world." "Stand back and look at the great rough-in plumbing job you just finished. Hey, pal, you did that?" Pride in the things you do, that's what sustains the motivation.

As of this writing, the United States is considering its options for dealing with the terrorists. By the time you read it, actions will have been taken and you will be reading history. No doubt any action will take understanding and cooperation by the American people. I have little doubt the president will find all the support he could ever want. Each of us feels we have been assaulted. We each want an action taken … our goal. I suspect, if asked, we will be willing to pay more taxes if that's what it takes. I'll be happy to pay. I will feel better if a definitive and decisive response is taken. That's what's in it for me!

A clear understanding of relevance to a goal cannot be overstated!

Fourth, activity. If you have all the other ingredients, but take no action to achieve your goal, you are not motivated, you will not find options, you are a spectator. If you choose not to act, reach for the channel changer, sit back and watch the electronic world pass in living color. You are a fake.

The sum total of who you were will be told in the works you leave behind. Your story is the trail of papers, buildings, children, pets, companies, books, objects, trees you leave behind. These too will fade, but the motivation you have to produce them is the thing that gives worth to your life today. It is in that motivation that we find reason to grab the tail of a full life. The only criterion for judging your life is in what you do. The only criterion for your motivation is what you do. To be is to act.

If other people are involved, start by having them take an action, any action towards achieving the goal. The best kind of initial action should be relatively simple, one clearly related to achieving the goal, one that can be completed with easy, but not simplistic effort, one where you can point to either a person or a team's effort, and one that can be publicized. The simple act of acting will encourage more action. Acts reinforce action. Once the action is completed, surprise. Without warning, reward your team or yourself. Out-of-the-blue rewards have an impact well beyond the nature of the reward itself. For small accomplishments, a bag of M&M's. For more, more. For a great deal more, a great deal more. Have fun with it. Remember, the single greatest motivator is recognition.

Working alone? Set a goal for the day. At the end of the day, go to the gym if you achieved the goal. At the end of the first chapter, a movie. Not until. We are all just animals. Reward our activity, we'll do it again. Ignore our activity and we'll frustrate you and ourselves out of our minds.

With these four elements in place, motivation is a snap, right? Sometimes. Motivation is not always clean and clear. Most of the time it's difficult to know the final source of your own motivation. You read an inspiring book on health, and you join a health club. Correct? No. You've read about health hundreds of times. Your friends have told you the value of diet and exercise. Why with this particular book did you make the decision to do something? What confluence of events pushed you over the edge? There is no easy or definitive answer.

Let's go back to the notion of *conditions for the possibility*. A month ago an old friend's wife had a slight heart attack. Disturbing, but alone not sufficient to warrant your joining a health club. Two weeks ago you were in an airport watching people. You noticed how many seem to be out of shape and were struggling with their bags. Necessary to help create the conditions for the possibility of your joining the health club, but not sufficient. Three days before you read the book, you were huffing and puffing up a small flight of stairs. Necessary but not sufficient. You read the book and all the elements came together in one blinding flash. Sufficient for you to see yourself as needing to do something. You were motivated. You took action.

Action is the only indicator of motivation.

Now for the Siamese twin to motivation. Passion.

How tall are you? Six feet. Easy.

Who are you? What moves you? What has meaning to you? How do you relate to other people? How do other people describe you? Not easy. You will never answer these kind of questions with "facts." You might describe yourself initially as a given height, a given weight, living at a given address. But that is not who you are. You really are the passions that form the subjective you. You love the sand at the beach, war movies, the sound of singing birds. What moves you and what has meaning to you is always laced with personal adjectives and abstract descriptions. These adjectives have no final meaning. They are phrased and rephrased in a thousand ways depending on your mood and the color of the day. Adjectives are the mercurial mosaic of a growing person. Facts are the static description of a couch potato.

It's in your passions and only in your passions that motivation arises. Passion is its motivation, its own reason. Passion knows how to let go of the tried and true and reach into a new and dark land. The reason is the passion, the passion is the reason. With passion, a fear becomes the adventure and we always return from the adventure wiser and changed.

Passion makes you sexy. Passions attract. Passions intoxicate. Passions subdue those who stray too close to the heat.

You are totally responsible for your passions. You are totally responsible for your emotions. You either control them or they control you. If you give in to their every desire, you end up on a rocky shore. If you fail to give into them you never come close enough to a rocky shore to experience the thrill of a close call. Steering between the two is the adventure and the challenge.

Each time you must choose, choose to steer close. Sailing far away debases and deadens the sound of the pounding sea.

A quiet universe is not for the motivated, not for the passionate.

Chapter 14
Courage

Although relegated to the number five position in this list, courage is often a kingpin of experience. A knowledgeable person may still not have the courage to make a move. "Move" is the key. Courage, like motivation, exists only in the actual doing of something. A courageous person doesn't sit on the sideline. If one is not going to take action toward finding options or gaining experiences, he is a shadow-boxer and fools only himself. Everyone around him sees he lacks courage.

What is courage?

Courage means taking direct action when facing the possibility of danger, pain, or difficulty. Direct action could be starting or joining a union, writing letters to editors on a ticklish subject, or attending PTO meetings and stating your point of view in direct opposition to the rest of the group. Direct action can also mean standing your ground against the tanks in Tienenmen Square or not attending a political rally when pressured to do so. Courage is manifested only in action.

In almost every conversation with people about their lives and why they have or have not achieved what they wanted, the reason seems always to come down to the amount of courage they did or did not have. Initially, most people will point to something like family responsibilities, money or a socially restrictive environment as a reason for their inaction. When pressed, they will admit that if they had just had the courage, they could have overcome these excuses and made the moves necessary to open options. These admissions come far too late for most. People often believe they have passed the point of no return and now the trek up the hill would be just too far. Another manifestation of the uncourageous. Another act of fear. Another act of self-denial.

There is never a point in anyone's life when it is too late to be courageous. In fact, the later in your life you decide to act, the less you have to lose. I recall one time I was giving a talk in New York State to a group of continuing education teachers. The average age was late 40s. I had just posed a question about how many of their political leaders had an "education" platform. Hands went up. Next, I asked how many of them had seen more money or more support for their teaching effort. No hands. I asked why they had not chosen to occupy the administration building or go on strike. One little lady in the front row shook her head and murmured that she was just too old. General agreement echoed around the room. I found it astounding that age had anything to do with courage. What better example of courage can be found than a person with age and wisdom standing up and saying, "This is not right, you won't get away with it!" If they are to be an example, let them lead by action, not by words. Action is courage and creativity manifested. If you are to find new options, you must have the courage to look for them. You must stand up and let them flow over you like a warm shower. You must be willing to be counted or you won't count.

Here's a challenge. The next time you are faced with a scary situation, ask this simple question: "If I just had a little more courage, what would I do?" Don't let yourself off with the easy answer, "I don't have enough courage, so there is no point in thinking about it." That's knee-jerk and shows a dearth of imagination and creativity. Let the question dwell with you for a few seconds. At the end of those seconds you will find there is really only one answer, "If I had enough courage, I would do what I want to do." Now, the only way out of inaction is to admit you lack courage. If that sits well with you, forget what it was you wanted and move on. You'll find more excuses along the way.

If, as should be the case, this lack of courage slams into your awareness like a hammer, then find new sources of courage and just damn the torpedoes and go for it. In the long run, what's the worst that will happen? You will likely be no worse off than you are right now. That's the downside. But the upside is you'll take control. Courage will win and you will begin establishing a new habit of treading where others won't.

Be sure and look yourself directly in the eye when you ask the question. It will put the responsibility where it belongs.

Motivation, passion and courage are all dynamically linked. The truly motivated, the truly passionate will always find the courage to open options. Courageous people are the envy of the world. Like the passionate, they too are the sexy ones, the ones with the guts to make things happen. They are the flame while most are the moths. They are the creative forces that make life more interesting for all of us.

The links between all six of these option-finding components are clear. If I am to be courageous, I must have the knowledge and understanding to pursue what I want. I also must have the health to be able to do so. Freedom is critical in exercising my courage. If I am in shackles, it is difficult to protest the banning of the book.

Without courage, there is no real person, only a silent shadow that drifts across the land and leaves nothing in its wake.

Chapter 15
Wealth

Far too often we miss life-affirming experiences because we don't have enough wealth. Really? Maybe. Sometimes. Most of the time it's an excuse. When I researched this book, wealth was always the last thing people mentioned when asked about the necessary elements for finding new options. Of course, this doesn't mean wealth is not important. In some cases it *is* the most important factor, while in similar cases the least. It's this contradiction that makes wealth so interesting.

What is wealth? Wealth is the external resources needed for accessing options.

Wealth is not who or what you are; how you use your options determines that. Wealth is outside the person you are. Notice that money alone, although mightily important, is not the only representation of wealth. Sometimes a great army may be the wealth needed to open an option. Friends that encourage, direct, or aid are manifestations of wealth. A borrowed book that enlightens is wealth. An automobile to get to work is wealth.... the list goes on. That being said, most of the things on this list can be bought with access to real money.

Wealth is anything but easy.

Wealth should never, never, never be underestimated.

Consider the other five components of options: freedom, health, knowledge, motivation, and courage. In very large part all five of these are available, in some degree, independent of wealth. I do not need wealth for freedom. I will indeed have more options available in my freedom if I have wealth, but it's not mandatory. Even if I'm destitute, I can still have health. Although I'll be in a better position to maintain my health if I have access to the food and shelter wealth provides, I can still be healthy as a horse while living in a tent. The same applies to knowledge, motivation and courage. You do better with wealth to back them up, but it's not absolutely necessary.

Contrast with just the single option of having wealth. In large part wealth is dependent on the other five components. It will be very difficult to grow in wealth without freedom, health, knowledge, motivation, and courage. Without knowledge, you won't know how to get wealth, or if you have some wealth, you won't know how to manage it. Without motivation, you'll have no drive to build wealth or maintain it. For the most part, the five components are necessary for wealth, but wealth is not totally necessary for them.

That being said, wealth comes as close as any of the six components to being sufficient in itself for opening options.

Consider. An aching tooth assumes priority over the money invested in a trip to Europe. But an expensive midnight excursion to the dentist can be bought, still permitting the trip to Europe. Wealth alone does not impart knowledge. But you can buy the best books, teachers, or tutors. You can be arrested and thrown in jail. But with enough money, you can buy your freedom from the law, even if you have killed your wife and her lover. You can be locked in a loveless relationship. But you can buy freedom with a divorce. You can't fly without wings. But you can buy a balloon and drift winglessly over the azure Aegean Sea. Wealth offers keys to many doors.

Under no circumstances should you underestimate the value and power of wealth.

There are some things wealth is not fully equipped to do.

Courage, in its raw form, cannot be bought. You can hire a mercenary to fight your battle or protect you. Think of the mob boss surrounded by lieutenants. That's mock courage. You can buy your way into a golden ghetto to protect life and limb, and not face the danger. That's mock courage. I can motivate you with money, but I can't buy you into a cause if it truly does not fit with your ethics and world view. Of course, few world views, few ethics are not without a price. Wealth will not overcome fooling with excuses. Freedom has nothing to do with how rich you are. Think of Howard Hughes.

With all the positive aspects of wealth, there is a dark side. Too much wealth can prove a deterrent to exploring new options. With enough money you may pay to have others do things for you, insulating yourself against the randomness of chance. Chance can add spice to many situations. With enough money you might take the easy route solving problems, never stretching yourself into the uncharted territory the lack of funds demands. When so much is easy and so accessible, you may find yourself unmotivated and uninspired to explore the many delights of things that can't be bought and sold.

Wealth comes in many forms and in many disguises. Because most of us confuse wealth with money, we fail to use our creativity when looking for other ways to open options. Innate ingenuity often proves a far greater asset than a fat bank account. The ability to parlay small sums into greater sums is wealth. The ability to sell an idea is far more decisive to an outcome than buying mercurial allegiance. A strike will bring money to its knees. The wealth of determined people, working in unison, is a wealth force of such significance that it has directed the world.

There is however one point that must be driven home again, and again and again: Never underestimate the power of money! If you don't have any, get some.

Perhaps that sounds far too glib. If it were that easy there would be no need for this chapter. But look around. As of this writing there is a negative saving rate in the United States. Credit card and general consumer debt is astronomical. Getting and holding money is difficult for most, impossible for others.

So let's assume you are not living in a second or third world country. Let's also assume you have some income. If you have read this far, you probably have a degree of interest in your future. With this in mind, how do you turn the glib statement "get some (money)" into a reality? Is there a process for accumulating money that will open options and experiences?

Yes, there are some basic rules that, if followed, will be instrumental in helping grow wealth. This list is in no way complete. That's impossible. Some of these rules you may already be following. Great. Others will need work and discipline, more discipline, and again, more discipline. Not one of these rules alone is sufficient to assure a pile of dough. Little is that easy. You will need to assess your current position and decide where you need work. You will also need to explore your commitment and your level of personal discipline. Without a true understanding of those two elements (they are the same coin) you will fail to reach any goal at all.

The following rules are in no order. If some sound trite and over-used, they are. If they sound like something you have heard before, you have. There is a vast amount of wisdom in many old saws. Your goal now is to remember them when you look at the coins in your hand or the bills in your wallet.

Rules for wealth:

1. Spend less than you make.
2. Save consistently. No matter what. Never backslide.
3. Learn the value of compound interest. Money over time makes more money.
4. Time has a dollar value.
5. Use credit cards wisely.
6. If you can't pay off your credit card at the end of the month, don't use it. Go without.
7. Always be willing to go without.
8. Beware of little expenses; small leaks will sink any budget.
9. Don't give into whining just to make peace. You'll lose the peace, the money, and the financial war.
10. Once a quarter, write down every penny you spend. Do so for three or four days. Make one day a Saturday. Review to determine if you are spending soundly.

11. If it sounds too good to be true, it probably is. Study before you invest.
12. Buy experiences wisely.
13. Don't delay investing in meaningful experiences today for fear of what you might not have tomorrow. Don't let the future hold you hostage. It has a funny way of arriving too late.
14. Big money does not come easily.
15. Neither a borrower (from friends) nor a lender (to friends) be. If you must lend, lend for a specific reason. Never lend for ongoing expenses. If they can't pay for them now, how will they be able to later? Help them find a way. If you lend the money, the debt is doubled.
16. Understand the value of things you can't own. Summer skies, passion, hand holding are free.
17. Invest in the five other options. They offer a great return.
18. Maintain quality associations. Birds of a feather profit together.
19. Wealth is what you enjoy, not what you own. Enjoy.
20. The most gain comes from the economical use of what you already have.
21. Debt is the worst poverty.
22. Slavery and debt ... synonymous.
23. Work hard and be willing to do what it takes. No job is beneath you if you have no options. Control your ego or it will starve you to distraction.

No doubt there are many more rules you can think of. Do so. Write them down and live by them until you have enough money to not worry about letting go of some of it. At that time, be magnanimous. It's one of the most fun things you can do.

Wealth: if you don't need it, it will make no difference to you. If you do need it and don't have it, it will make all the difference to you.

Chapter 16
Five Questions.
One Statement.

As indicated throughout this book, the only thing that counts is your action. The rest is noise. The challenge then is how to use the six components to enhance and expand your experiences.

Analyze.

Each time an interesting experience presents itself, review the following five big questions and one statement. Somewhere in this analysis is the answer ... If you really want it.

Big Question 1: Is this experience one you think would be worth reliving?

If so, what in it makes you think so? Is it unique to the experiences you normally have? Is that important to you? Does it offer a gain in knowledge or opportunities that you would like to add to your life? Does it force you to go against the grain? Can you make a buck? Are you unhappy about all the other experiences you have missed? Figure out why you want the experience and other things fall into place.

It was my friend Wayne Hunter who suggested I hitchhike across central Africa. At the time he worked for Pan Am. I considered what I would gain from such a trip and told him to book it. I would be alone, but thought this would be a trip I would delight in re-living and re-telling again and again. I could have applied a host of criteria to arrive at the decision but most would have been reasons not to go. I thought only about the reason to go. I went and the only time I look back with any regret was in Kampala, Uganda, when I spent four days in bed with malaria. So what! I would gladly do the whole trip again … even with the delirium.

An example: let's assume you have the opportunity to hike into the Grand Canyon. It is an experience you would like to have.
Statement:
But, I can't have this experience because options are not open to me.
You are too out of shape to trek down to the Grand Canyon.

Big Question 2: Which of the six components prevents the option from being open to me?
Clearly, a health issue. There may be others, but to keep it simple, let's stick with health.

Big Question 3: What is missing in that component?
You smoke and carry many extra pounds.

Big Question 4: What can I do to fill the missing part of that component?
Stop smoking, get on an exercise program, lose weight.

Big Question 5: When this experience is actually open, will you go for it or make an excuse?
This final question is far and away the most difficult. You must chose, either you do or you don't. Can the choice be any simpler? Can the decision be any more personal? The Grand Canyon awaits.

If there are interacting components, deal with each of them individually. Based on your analysis, make an action plan. Keep at it. The more you analyze, the more ideas come and the more excuses you'll clear away.
You can always find new ways to have life-affirming experiences. If not you, who? You can always find new reasons not to. It's up to you.

⏳

Chapter 17

Break Point

You stand at the edge of the dark abyss. By now a great deal is clear. You're clear on the result you want for your life, A life worth repeating. Clear that repeatable experiences are sufficient for that result. Clear that a full range of options are sufficient for these experiences to happen. Clear that each of the six components is necessary for finding these options. You have examined each component and are clear on where you are strong, where you are weak and what you must do to gain full strength in all six arenas. The clarity of total personal responsibility churns deep inside. The ultimate power, your options, has grown into a clear vision of the life-affirming person you intend to be.

Now you face crossing the dark abyss. The abyss of fear. The fear of actually taking the kind of actions that usher new experiences into reality. Here you finally come face to face with all the ingrained excuses and prohibitions that have plagued you and dictated your life up to this very second. Here you must do more than want reliable experiences, you must jump the abyss and take specific actions. It's only on the other side of the abyss that change takes place.

Welcome, you are at the Break Point.

Break Point is a special time on your journey when the theory of new experiences and the reality of acting on that theory meet. Here, you are alone, face to face with everything you've read and everything inside that wants out. Here you either take the risk or walk way. It's here where you are master of your fate or a pawn. At no other point are you confronted with the reality that you make or don't make excuses. At Break Point your past world and the world of new experiences collide. One will win, one will lose.

To proceed.

There is a term in physics called the "elsewhere." If an errant Martian flipped a switch, turning off the sun, it would take about eight minutes for the last photons leaving the sun to hit the earth. After that, darkness. That unique period of time between the switch turning off the sun and darkness is called the "elsewhere." The time between the event itself and the knowledge of the event. There is a mystery around the term that forms a delightful image in one's mind. It can also be the very heart of Break Point. Next time you are standing at the abyss, facing a decision about a potential, life-affirming, unique, and challenging experience, stop. That decision point is the event, the moment the sun goes out.

Pause.

Don't give in to the knee-jerk reaction that has been such a part of your decision-making process in the past.

Pause.

Pause. Pause for an extraordinary moment. Spend just a little time in the "elsewhere," that time before you make a decision. Let the potential of the experience wash over you like a wave of brilliant light. Look down into the dark abyss with your new clarity. Look deep. Determine what's down there. Is it real, or a cloudy demon from the past with sharp talons and teeth? Vapor and fantasy? Is it all the unfounded prohibitions and mythical punishments of days gone by? Just think about it. This pause may be the difference between a repetition and an adventure.

Look over at the far side of the abyss. You now have a choice. Jump or not. Take the risk or not. Go for the experience with the prospect of tumbling into the imagined abyss or not.

Pause.

Jumping or not jumping, acting or not acting is not the intent of Break Point. Break Point is simply the pause, the critical interlude you spend in the "elsewhere," considering your options. In that fanciful and pregnant moment, your objective is to understand that it's not *what* you choose, it's *why* you make one choice over another. That's the key to Break Point working for you. Understanding why you choose what you do. If you choose not to jump to a new experience for fully considered reasons that's fine. If the choice not to jump is for unconsidered, knee-jerk reasons—"my mama always told me not to," "what would the neighbors say?" "I just never think that way." "It's a sin"— alarms should go off all around you. You aren't digging deep enough. Reflexive responses should find no refuge in you. Your quest is different.

Break Point is a very special time. Your time. The time when you realize that if you don't expect the unexpected, it will not happen to you. It's the time when you decide never to say no when you really want to say yes, yes to all the experiences that could be life-enhancing.

An awareness from a new perspective.

You jumped over the abyss; an act of true personal authenticity, perhaps one of the first sincere acts you have made for a long time. It took courage, didn't it? Now you'll need even more courage to stay with your decision and to continue making decisions based on personal authenticity. Beware of the ease with which you can backslide. The terrain on the far side of the abyss is murky and filled with unknowns. It will take some time for eyes and body to grow accustomed. Give it the time it needs. Don't let inattention creep in and send you back to the undifferentiated average everydayness. Stick with pausing at break-point. Stick with weighing your options. Stick with not giving in to the knee-jerk answer and actions. Stick with the result you want from your life.

All we have is time. Vast sums vanish and vaporize in excuses and catastrophic expectations. Before the time is all used up, take a small chunk of it and use it for the "elsewhere." It may change the course of the rest of your life.

Chapter 18
The Phenomenon of the Apostrophe 'T'

The sliding doors of the hotel restaurant were open to the aromatic air of an intoxicating June night in Miami Beach. Multicolored tubes of deco neon twisted luminescently into flamingos and spirals of phantasmagoria.

The woman sat at a table about four feet away from me. She had just finished eating. The waiter came over to clear the dishes.

"How was your dinner?"

Without looking up, she said: "You should have brought the salad earlier. I was unhappy that it came with the meal."

Unhappy? Unhappy about what? She had eaten the entire meal, including the salad, and now she was unhappy about something that was finished, passed, history, never to be visited again. The salad can never "should have been brought earlier." Unhappy? Why had she chosen to be unhappy about that? What exactly did she think would be the result of that unhappiness? Perhaps she thought the waiter could run the film backwards, stop at a specific point, bring the salad, then start the film again. Without a neo-Einsteinian gizmo for changing the laws of the universe, her request exposed only one thing... a person who likes to bitch about things. There was nothing the waiter could do, so all she might have achieved was a childish way to justify reducing the tip. If that was the case then she was not only a bitch but a coward, too gutless not to leave a tip at all. Either way, she lost.

There are three phases in the life of all humans: the past, the present, and the future. Of the three, you have a modicum of actual, hands-on control over two: the present and the future. The operative word is "modicum." An errant asteroid can nullify the future with no warning, and the present nanosecond is subject to change by an inattentive driver at the next traffic light. Control of the present and future is always doubtful, but creative activity in that direction is the best we've got. The past, however, is completely out of our sway. Once the sand has passed the neck of the hourglass, there is no way it can find its way back to the top to run down again. It's true however, that the past is always magnanimously open for review and new interpretation. In some cases, a new interpretation of the past is the genesis of a healthy present and enraptured future, but there is no act you can take to change what actually transpired.

What does this have to do with the salad lady under the deco neon glow?

She focused on the wrong things, she injured her eating experience, and she made herself unhappy.

How?

First, she invested her energy and time in something over which she had no control. Unless she planned on eating at that restaurant on another night, having the same waiter, and having a salad, she accomplished nothing except making herself, the waiter, and me (better never to eavesdrop) uneasy. She could not change history. The salad was gone. The delivery had been made. Nothing positive could result from her statement.

Second, at that point she proved herself to be impotent and irresponsible. Her intent was not to take control. Had responsibility been involved, she would have asked for the salad at the start, or asked that the next time she eats there the salad be brought first; or if she were passing through, she might have just shut up. As a responsible and potent person, she would have been keenly aware she couldn't change the past. Because she chose to complain about the past, she broadcast, "I CAN'T CONTROL SO I'LL COMPLAIN! I'M

IMPOTENT AND IRRESPONSIBLE AND I'LL INFLICT MY IMPOTENCE AND IRRESPONSIBILITY ON YOU BECAUSE THERE IS NOTHING YOU CAN DO ABOUT IT EITHER! I'LL POINT THE FINGER OF RESPONSIBILITY AWAY FROM ME AND TOWARD YOU, AND I'LL MAKE YOU SUFFER WITH ME! I'M STUPID."

Third, she reinforced her own victimization. "Oh, poor me, they didn't bring my salad earlier. People always do that to me. There's just nothing I can do about it."

The problem is deeper than a lady, a salad, a waiter. It has to do with agent, blame and responsibility.

As I mentioned, at age two I had polio. It left me with a delightfully smaller right leg and a wonderful, sexy limp. At some point in my development I realized that other people were not like me. I didn't hold that against them, it was just what had happened to them. I did, of course, wonder how people described them to a blind date, but that was not my problem. As I became more aware of the agent, blame, responsibility trilogy, I began to notice people blaming an agent for their not having my sexy limp. They also blamed this agent for their not being able to run as slowly as I, and for not being able to trip and fall with the grace and composure I exhibited at all times. It was not unusual to see my friends whipped into an animated and vitriolic froth as they lashed out, blaming the agent for their deficiency. Often I would find them hiding away, embarrassed by their shortcomings.

One lucky day a friend's mother told him that although this agent had not smiled on him, and had indeed dealt him a bad hand, it was done. The hand had been dealt and blame would yield nothing but baleful moans and wishful impossibilities. She said to him, "forget the agent, it has no relevance to the situation." Her final question to him was, "Now that polio is gone and you can't have it, exactly who are you going to blame for your deficiency?" My friend suddenly realized he could no longer point the finger of responsibility toward any agent. The finger could only be pointed back at him, toward his resentment, toward his unwillingness to take the kind of action that would give him the sexy limp. I lost contact with that friend but I suspect that he took a drastic action to achieve his goal.

The agent may have been the cause of your current situation, but the agent in no way has the responsibility to get you out of it. Even if the agent is ethical and extends a hand, it is still your responsibility to take it or reject it. The agent is a bystander in this decision-making process and is allowed in only if you allow it.

Enter the phenomenon of the apostrophe "T."

The phenomenon of the apostrophe "T" distinguishes two statements:

It can't be different
It can be different

The only difference between these two statements is the apostrophe "T." What has happened can't be changed. What you do with what's happened and the impact it has over you can be changed.

I recall a story of a woman whose son drowned more than a decade ago. Clearly a tragedy. Within a few months of his death, she had decided to become an alcoholic and a recluse. To this day, she drinks heavily, has ruined her health, and wallows in such despair that she has alienated her other kid and all of her good friends. At some point her good friends told her to get on with things. Her not good friends continued to support her grimness for a while with hollow, feel-good, words like "ah, yes, I know how you feel," and "it takes time." At some point even the not-good friends drifted away because they could lie for only so long. Now she is left with a bottle and a misguided belief that with enough grief and sorrow, the tide of events will change and the dead child will return. He won't! He's gone. He's not coming back. It can't be different and all the grief and sorrow in the world will not change that.

It can be different.

Recognize the death and its finality. Move as smoothly as you can through the grieving process, pick up the meaningful pieces, and get on with life. Now, don't throw the book down and accuse me of being unsympathetic. I understand sympathy, and am the first to provide support in times of need. That is not the point. Cataclysmic events need recovery time. Only to a point.

There are people who have been divorced for years, but are still harboring such debilitating anger and hostility that they are unable even to think about or speak to their ex without a pronounced physical or psychological reaction. Why? What's served? It's past. Is that hostility going to change anything? Will the kids benefit from such rancor? Will anyone's life be easier or more fulfilled? Will this yield new options and experiences worth reliving? No! Grow up and get your ego out of it.

An attorney once told me how much money he makes on domestic cases. Within the first hour, he said, he can tell the client exactly what will happen in the case. He's almost always right. At some point, the vindictive and retaliatory ego of either one or both of the parties enters the arena, and logic and rationality exit through the back door. Cash for the attorney flows in through the front. The lawyer sees it coming but no matter how he tries to still the hysterical ego, it will not be pacified until both parties are bled dry of cash and psychic energy. If one person wants out of a relationship, let it go and get on with it. If both want to work on it, work on it, but if it isn't working, cut the loss, work to be friends and get back to living.

A study was done some time ago to determine what made people unhappy. If I recall the statistic, more than 80% of everyone's unhappiness was due to something that happened in the past, something over which they now have no control. "He left me." "I lost all my money in that business." "I come from an abusive family." "My father was a drunk." Not one of these things can be changed. It can't be different, but it can be different if one decides to learn from the past, understand the injury and pain, and deal with the situation in a new light.

Don't misunderstand. You should not forget the past. Much to the contrary. All of those past pains and pleasures make you who you are. The key is not to wallow in the past or let it keep you from becoming who you can be.

A trip down memory lane is one of the most delightful trips you can make. Avoid the sticker bushes.

And in the day-to-day moments of your life·

The traffic is locked up. The plane is late. The hotel room is not ready. The computer is down. The car won't start.

If you are not a traffic cop, prop your feet up. No one wants to hear you complain about something you can't control.

Are you an air traffic controller, or do you control the weather? No? Watch it snow.

Are you willing to make the bed, clean the toilet? No? Watch people.

Can you fix the computer? No? Write in your notebook.

Fix your car? No? Watch the sunset.

If there is nothing you can do about the current situation, don't complain. Complaining alone never does any good. It's a child of weakness. Who wants to hear it? Sit back, take a deep breath and find some creative way to occupy your mind. Or, you can watch all the other people get worked up about things they can't control. You'll be amazed at just how silly they look in this futile endeavor.

Learn what you can't control—it can't be different.

Learn what you can control—it can be different.

A word of caution. Once you realize the past is truly gone and nothing you do will change it, you'll have a more stoic attitude toward the vicissitudes of life. You'll find you're able to accept the bad things as a way of the world, and you'll find you don't get worked up to the degree people may expect. This will prove difficult. For some reason, when bad things happen, there is a level of emotion that people seem to feel appropriate. Fall short, and you appear to be, at best, unfeeling, at worst an emotional clod. Most likely, this is not a problem with you, but rather with those around you who are unable to understand the delightful mixture of joy and sorrow. In the vast majority of cases, rampant emotional outbursts and long-term grieving are attempts to change the world back to the way it was. They are also ways to control you! With enough tears and gnashing of teeth, things will be righted. The dead will return. The lover will come back. The company won't go bust.

The tears will change nothing. The best way to deal with grief and loss is to accept it, let the feeling out and get on with it. Anything beyond that is a misguided belief that life is always good, kind, and fair. It's a belief held by anyone unwilling to see the full flow of human reality and accept it as inevitable.

The world will deal good hands. The world will deal bad hands. The world does not care how you handle it. It makes no difference whether you are debilitated by it or take it in stride. Only you can care to apologize for something you have done. Only you can take an action to right what you think wrong. The world is impartial.

It's your choice how you handle it.

It always is.

Chapter 19
What to Choose

What to do? What to do?

Our most difficult challenge: what to do with this temporal blink of an eye? Deceiving ourselves about our limitations and restrictions can consume a huge chunk of our time and energy. We cover desires and wishes with dubious reasons for inaction. At some point, we look around and wonder where all that time went.

The sadness of it all.

But the most remarkable aspect of a human being is the tremendous power of inner determination. A person with a clear idea and a burning determination to realize a creative goal will surmount almost any obstacle in reaching his or her goal.

Those who know what they want will become the great and the near great.

Sadly this is not the fate of most of us. Gradually the grand, shining, and ambitious plans and imaginings of youth dim, then are opaqued over with the rush of daily life and the indifference of the ever-elusive tomorrows. We are left with mortgages, credit card bills, and only vague notions of what might still captivate, enthrall, transfix us. The mundane overwhelms; we retreat, believing greatness or near greatness is not our lot.

It's a lie.

At a foggy point and for a muddy reason, we learned to believe that only the great achieve great things. But how is that so? By what measure of greatness? By whose coordinates? Exactly what magnitude of great does something have to be to be relegated to that hallowed position called greatness? Is greatness a historical footnote or a terrific casserole? Is greatness a walk on the moon or a walk out of a hospital? Because we've bought into the current definition of greatness, along with its hollow and often obscene trappings, most of us feel excluded. We don't fit the definition. We fail to search for our own personal re-definition, electing instead to add another layer of opacity to our dreams. The distance to *their* definition is too far. Greatness is for others.

What is your greatness? What must you do to define yourself? How do you extricate those things from all the layers of muck heaped upon us by sincere or fraudulent map-makers? How do you overcome your own apathy? How do you sift through the vague and sometimes conflicting notions of greatness to find your own? How do you winnow away what "they" say and what "they" think until all that's left is the essence of what you think? How do you really understand what you want out of a repeatable life, your own, very special passion?

Drink from the river.

A refresher in mythology:

You die. Your soul is whisked away to the underworld. You stand confused in a strange land on the muddy bank of the river Styx. The river flows, unreal and iridescent. There is no sound...nothing.

"Over here!" a voice breaks the silence. "Hurry up!" Charon, the raggedy old man, in an uncertain boat waves you to a rickety wooden landing. You get in the boat. He paddles you silently across the river.

On the far side Cerberus, the three-headed dog guarding the underworld, howls and snarls, closing the path behind.

"Stand close," Minos says. The three judges of Hades review your life. Your sentence is passed, you continue down the path. Your strange and astonishing journey is about to end. Just one more thing, you'll have to drink from Lethe, the river of forgetfulness.

You approach. The river is mirror still. You lean down and carefully fill the cup. The water sparkles. You lift the cup and prepare to drink, knowing all worldly remembrances will be swept away.

"Wait." Prometheus, lover of man, interrupts.

"Before you drink," he tells you, "there is one thing you must know. The sparkling water of Lethe will wash away all your earthly memories...except—" He pauses. "—Except the memory of all the experiences you wanted in your earthly life but couldn't find the courage to have. Those absent memories should have been part of your greatness, but you never let them in. Now, they'll find a permanent home deep within you, haunting and tormenting you for all the rest of time. Nothing you can do will ever remove them from your spirit as it wanders ceaselessly here on the homeless plain of Asphodel."

You watch the sparkling water. Unrequited desires dance in the rippling surface. Hopes, vague wishes, and regrets dance in your head as you remember all the times you said "next time." A haunting "next time."

Finally you understand.

Life doesn't go on forever. If it did, our actions would have no importance at all. If you don't do it now, you can always do it later. Nothing need animate you, there is nothing you have to do before you die. Death won't happen. If you don't taste the wine or feast on the banana pudding while it's here, no matter, you can feast an eon, or two, or ten from now, it'll be there. In this infinite existence, what makes any time or any place important? Nothing!

Spatiotemporal: The here, the now. The primary punctuation mark for living.

But there's more dread hiding in that endless life: your very disappearance. Whatever you do during this eternity can have no unique qualities, it's been done thousands of times in the past. Your actions blend in with the actions of all the rest. Your potential is everyone's potential. Nothing will be yours, and the unique actions that encompass you have no extraordinary merit, they encompass everyone. The reflection of all of us, like the one in the barber chair, reflects endlessly and no single reflection is different from any other.

Who are you in that reflection?

The shape of who we are, what we make of ourselves, our uniqueness is bounded by a terminator.

The shape of anything is determined by a boundary. Without that end point, we lack form and identity. I am everyone. I am no one. You are everyone. You are no one. With a clear understanding of this end point, it's easier to walk away from the mirror and make your own reflection during your time. Dance to a new melody, one that is a reflection of you, not of others.

A story without an ending is not a story.

At that moment of death, we are what we are. That's it. It's over. Your story is told. No one will interpret your future actions or your intentions. This realization gives us the strength for vital living. The radical awareness of "not being" changes being into an exciting momentary blink of the eye, a time to fill with life-affirming experiences.

But you're not standing on the bank of the river Styx. You've not been judged. You're not about to lift the cup of forgetfulness to your lips. Yet there is the Promethean warning and there is still time to heed it... not a mythological time but a real time. A now time. A time of opportunity.

Here are some questions:

What regrets would you not want roaming around in your head and haunting you forever?

What experiences would you fear missing, knowing that their absence would burden you for all of eternity?

What tradeoffs are you making? (It's always a question of tradeoffs.)

Are these tradeoffs the ones you really want to make or are you closing off options to keep the peace? We all have to give up on some options during the tradeoff. It's the way of life.

How much are you giving up during the peace conference?

Do you resent the outcome or is it within reason? This is a question only you can answer. Don't just pass over these questions and read on. Think very carefully. Did you always want to write a novel? How about a sailing trip around Greece? The photography class you never found time to take? The hour a night you wanted to read to your kid? Each of these "should have's" will rattle around in your eternal head like so many marbles because you never found the time or courage to make the move. So, what are the things that you most want to do? What would you regret not having done? I think of Athens. I remember Helen.

You have one tool: **Eternal regret.**

You are sitting by the river Lethe, cup in hand, contemplating the magnitude of spending all the rest of time regretting the things you didn't do. But there is no clarity. The edges are soft and a clear conclusion about what you would regret hangs just out of reach. Perhaps sharpening the focus will help, providing a plan of action today...

What causes someone to act? The prospect of personal gain. No one ever acts against their actual or perceived self-interest. *I* generate all altruistic actions. *I* give them merit. *I* weigh the consequences. *I* will decide what must be done. There is no external agent in this final decision. Anonymous donors give because giving makes them feel good. Suicide may seem a better option than a life of physical or psychic pain that appears to have no end.

What causes someone not to act? The gain doesn't seem worth the effort. "Things are OK, why make a change?"

The problem with this notion of "current conditions" is that we fail to understand that there can be a ruinous cumulative aspect. Something may not be so bad now, but what if the condition continues year after year? Sure, it may not seem so bad then either, but what have you lost? What nags at you in the night? After almost 30 years of marriage, how much did you compromise for fear of being alone or fearing the loss of security? Did you just drift through and let too much slip away? Did it fall apart all around you and the best you could come up with was "yes, but?" It's in the "yes, but's" that we find the regret of a life not lived. It is also here that we find resentment.

Resentment: A tool for action.

Remember, resentment is never about "them," it's always about you. You don't resent the "current condition" for what it did to you, you resent yourself and the simple fact that you were not strong enough to change it. You didn't have the right training, so you resented the fact that you were passed over for the promotion. You didn't resent the big client who insisted you lower your price, you resented yourself for getting into such a vulnerable position. Or, perhaps you were powerless, so you assumed a moral high ground. You one-upped them: "You are a sinner and although I may not be able to conquer you now, you just wait till the next life, I'll sit by and watch you burn. God will take care of you." Resentment run amok.

Resentment: Use it.

What do you resent? Who do you resent? By giving consideration to these questions, you'll find areas of personal weakness, areas where you can improve and take pro-active control of your future. If you resent the guy or gal who just got the promotion, forget the resentment and ask yourself what they did to get promoted. What can you do so you will get the promotion next time? If you resent the friend who's asked to parties when you are not, decide what to do to improve your social skills and networking. If you resent your friends' trip to Paris or the month in India, cut your expenses, save your money, plan your time and take a trip yourself. The time you spend on resentment can be better used in improving yourself.

Resentment can be a rich vein of opportunity if you examine it through a proactive lens, as opposed to indulging in a reactive grudge.

Find what you resent and make it work for you. It's that easy.

Go back over this section. Substitute the word "envy" for "resentment." They are the same color.

You have a second tool.

Stress and distress, another tool for action.

The world is full of stress. A great deal is good. It gets us going and keeps things hopping. Some is painful, and we carry it inside, aware or unaware that it's nibbling away at us. At some point the stress takes a dreadful or wonderful leap and turns into distress. This distress replaces the nibbling *at* us with eating *into* us. It's here, if we are self-aware enough, that we act…it's in our conscious self-interest to do so. Stress we can deal with, distress moves us to a new level.

With enough courage and desire, we eliminate the distress or reduce it to an acceptable level. This reduction/elimination of distress becomes a motivating goal unto itself. In fact, it can become an illness, so overwhelming that every other activity falls away and our daily life revolves around eliminating this distress. Think of a painful situation, you break your foot. Clearly distressing. The initial pain and distress over the situation is such that it blocks out all other activities. You are confined to bed, then to crutches. Almost all your focus is on the problem. After a few days you began to deal with the pain and the inconvenience. You quickly learn how to negotiate steps, take a shower, and drive, because you have to get back to work. Each of these adaptive activities is new because they require unusual ways to accomplish old ends. The pain and the inconvenience have taught you things that previously never would have never been considered much less tried. If the break is extremely bad you may have to use a walking aide for the rest of your life. More distress. You turn that distress into a learning opportunity and find new ways of accommodating. The distress became the motivator to learn and take action, a teacher in the school of hard knocks. Strangely, it's here that we realize some of our best creativity and enterprise. Use it.

In some cases we will do almost anything to escape and keep ourselves from falling back into the distressful condition that dominated our life. If we are healthy, we take charge of distress and make a change. If we are unhealthy, it will take charge of us and we might rob or kill for the next fix. Or, often, if we seek help, the medical profession suggests only pharmacological solutions. We then find ourselves "justifiably" eliminating all distress. That path becomes a slippery slope.

There's gold in distress. Make it work for you.

Remember, your objective is to enjoy life. That being understood, the strategy now is to turn selected stresses in your life into distresses. In this transformation you will find new driving goals and the courage to act on them. An example: you want to take a two-week vacation to Paris. Your stress comes from working too hard and not taking the necessary time for yourself. Now your work has you in a toxic spiral that seems to have no exit. Paris looms large as a beguiling, unattainable, and frustrating goal. You find yourself strung-out by the demands of work, family, commitments. Your time is not your own and you feel the stress of never seeing Paris.

Elevate your stress. Say to yourself: "I'll *never* see Paris. I will always wonder what it would have been like to walk along the Seine and flood all my senses with the echoes of Hugo, Baudelaire, Monet, DeSade, DeGaulle. All of this will pass me by and I will be left, sitting by Lethe, with "it might have been." The more you focus on what you'll miss, the more inspirited life you give to the stress of missing Paris, and the more you will elevate your emotional state into distress. The closer you come to distress, the more likely you are to act. Remember, we make almost all of our decisions on an emotional basis, and defend them on a rational basis. Let your emotions lead you to Paris. Let your emotions and the core understanding of "It's now or never" take you to a new level of desire. It's then you'll find a rational way to make it work. That's what we do best!

The caution.

Enter into the duality of resentment and distress with a clear awareness that it can turn to quicksand. When you acknowledge a resentment or elevate a stress to distress, act at once. If you let these new emotions fester and grow, they can overwhelm you and you will find yourself even more repressed and frustrated. Like everything else in life, the key is acting, not simply wallowing and observing. To move toward an active solution as opposed to over-analysis and endless ruminating is the key to achieving your goals.

Now you have three tools: the river Lethe, resentment and distress. The choice of using them is still and always will be up to you.

⌛

Chapter 20

How to Choose

Ushering in a new order of living demands courage and risk. The tendency is often to stay on a current well-trodden path, shying away from one that's littered with unknowns and punctuated by our own catastrophic expectations. The simple fact, however, is that as long as we are conscious, there is absolutely no choice. but to choose. Choosing to do nothing and remain on the same straight path is a choice, even if you don't see it as one. Deny as you might, you are never free of the structural responsibility for the conscious actions you take or do not take, even within the extreme limits of the "circumstance" of your life. It's a real circumstance that you can't drink up the sea or simply hop out of abject poverty. It's not at all a real circumstance that you can't think about it, and work toward these impossible objectives no matter how minute the action, how futile or how remote the chances of success.

It's important, however, to realize when you have no choice. There are circumstances that may prevent a person from recognizing or fantasizing about any option. I recall all too clearly a photograph of tiny child in Ethiopia bent over, face in the hot sand, near death. A buzzard stood nearby in hungry attendance. The child had no consciousness of the world. Choice had no place in his horizon or in the arid, windswept desert of his mind. He would die. There are two times when you have no choice: when you are dead or unconscious.

So, in our case, the option of not choosing is delusional, a lie of the highest magnitude. Nothing outside you determines your final decision. Nothing. You choose from within the situation in which you find yourself. You can either choose to run from the burning house or stay. Eat the cake or pass. Believe in god or not. Even if you "accept Jesus as your savior," or adopt an ascetic way of life, you are still required to choose continuing to do so even if you believe that the path is fixed and illuminated by divine intervention. You still have the option of interpretation, and in that interpretation you can and will change any perspective into what you choose. Even under the most hideous duress, you still have a choice in the way you think.

So we must make a choice, and in that choice we sacrifice the possibilities of all other choices existing at that moment. Since we can do only one thing at a time we must try to choose the one thing with the most positive experiential potential.

Here inertia and resistance can set in. With such a vast array of options, it is often far less risky to choose to stay with what we know, even if it ain't so good.

Time passes. The tide slips out un-noticed. Many life-affirming experiences spin in the eddy, are sucked down and drowned.

Why does this happen to us?

We hold a convoluted reality when it comes to change. Change is scary. But more often than not, actually reaching into the dark unknown seldom matches the catastrophic expectations we have of what goblin lurks there. We believe the neighborhood won't be good, the power will fail, the traffic will jam, the air won't support our wings, we'll be abandoned.

We retreat.

Most of the time these morose speculations are bogus. In fact, the move into this dark new territory is often exhilarating, heightening our awareness of the world and magnifying our place in it. We feel renewed and recharged. So why do we shy away? Because we aren't sure, and surety is security; we are willing to sacrifice a great deal for security, even our involvement in the world.

Security is an illusion. It's the sand lifted off the top of a dune during a strong wind. Involvement in the world is factual. It's the noisy parade down Main Street with brass and drums.

But that's not good enough. To say that security is illusory doesn't relieve the need for it. We blunder into believing that there's too much to lose. Sometimes there is. Sometimes there isn't. Most of the time the latter. What to do?

Analyze.

Most of us respond well when we have a clear understanding of risk. If we can see what we stand to lose with respect to what we have to gain, we are better able to arrive at a meaningful decision. "Just having a feeling" about something may or may not serve us in our decision making. Although "gut feeling" is one of the most powerful tools in our arsenal of decision making (treat it with utmost respect), it can always use a bit of data to help it along. Wouldn't it be nice if there was a qualitative and a quantitative way to aid your gut in determining if you want to take the risk?

Try this.

On the top of a piece of paper write down the experience you want. Be as specific as you can. The experience can be anything from deciding to move to a new city, taking a new job, getting into or out of a marriage, or starting your own business.

Next, on another piece of paper, think of all the reasons you have for wanting this experience. Again, be specific. If, for example, you want to start your own business, some of the reasons may be to be your own boss, to have the freedom you want to express yourself, to keep more of the money you now make for others. Keep listing until you feel you have covered the most important points. Next, look at each of the points and determine exactly how important they are to you. This is strictly a subjective scale about how you feel. On a 1 to 100 scale, give each of the reasons a numerical rating of its importance to you and how you want to live. If you want to open your own business, and one reason is to be your own boss …you really want to be your own boss, you might give that desire a 90 or 95. If you like the idea of freedom, you might give it a 50. Think about each point and decide its value to you. This will tell you a great deal about what you really want and how important it is.

You now have two columns. A list of reasons to try something new and a subjective value for each.

On another sheet of paper make a list of all the reasons not to take the action. Again, if you want to start a business, your investment might be $100,000. One risk might be losing that money. Another might be not making enough money to send your kids to college. List all the reasons you think important for not taking the action. Once the list is complete, start with the first concern, and, again on a 1 to 100 scale, determine exactly how bad (the catastrophe factor) it would be if your concern actually came to pass. If you lost the $100,000 would it be ruinous: 100, or would it be a set-back: 60? By examining each of your concerns in this light, you are forced to analyze if the catastrophe has legitimate power or is only a phantom with no teeth.

The final step is to look at each of the concerns you have listed along with the catastrophe factor to determine how likely it is that the catastrophe will actually occur. This is called the probability factor and it is expressed as a percentage. In the example of opening your own business, your concern was that you would lose your money if the business failed. Well, how likely is it that the business will fail? In some cases there are places you can go to get factual information. If you are opening a dog grooming business, you can find statistics on the success rate of those kinds of operations. Without that direct info, you can again use your gut and put a percentage beside the potential catastrophe. In the case of the dog grooming business, your research tells you that 10% of these businesses fail. You now know that the chances of losing your investment is only 10%. Armed with that information, you are in a better position to make a more rational decision.

Now here's the fun part of the exercise. Let's assume that the catastrophe factor for losing your money is 75. Important, but not ruinous. The probability of failure is very low, only 8%, but you still feel that's too high. You would be much more comfortable and willing to take the risk if that were 5%. Now your creative objective is to shave three points off the probability so you can proceed with the action. In our dog grooming case, you could attend a business class at the local community college, you could go to work for a groomer, you could hire a consultant, you could take on a partner. If you did one or two of these things, you might easily shave off the needed points to move forward. The key is that you are not stifled and confused by having no benchmark or "hard" information upon which to base this decision. Without some clear measurement, we tend to retreat into the safety of the tried and true in lieu of exploring the new.

If you and your partner need to decide something, try this technique. It will uncover points of concern and fear that can be addressed and a course of action planned. Without this, you'll be tilting at nebulous windmills.

I have a friend whose husband is ill. Recently, they were trying to decide whether to accept a new course of treatment. It was not an easy decision because this particular treatment has a significant life-threatening downside. One night, after having done a great deal of research they sat down, and using this technique they balanced out their information. They then decided not to have the procedure. This was not just a balance of one treatment against another but a balance of to do or not to do based on a comprehensive study of the facts. By using this technique they came to a "rational" decision that felt comfortable to both. With the rational part under their belt, they made the final decision based on the all-important gut feel. A wonderful mixture of the rational and intuitive. Right now things have worked out fine for him. Even if things had not worked out for the best, they would have both felt better about things because of the way the decision had been made.

Never forget that even with the best measurement nothing is guaranteed. If you are looking for that, stay in bed, cover your head and hope. You're expecting too much and you're missing the fun. Instead, take some time to judge the potential pros and cons of an experience, then make allowances and adjustments where needed. This process will make it harder to delude yourself about why it shouldn't be tried or is filled with danger. Moving to action will become a great deal easier.

Besides, what's the worst that can happen?

It probably won't! If it does, adjust. You can't adjust something that is not happening.

Chapter 21
Sex and Experience

This chapter does not belong in this book. On some levels it violates many of the considerations put forth so far. It gives strong precepts, rules and beckons at things to do and things not to do. It is included because it exemplifies the kind of considerations that are part of living like you mean it. Read it with a different eye, an open and at ease mind. As with the whole of the book, it should be provocative and send you into new territory. It may jar you a bit—at least I hope so.

That is the point of all of this, isn't it?

We all miss repeatable experiences in a myriad of ways, and in a multitude of situations. That's a given. But there is one area where missing experience seems ubiquitous and rampant: sex.

Sex has more bogus social and religious taboos and prohibitions than just about any other activity. People who believe these rules may well buy into the same kind of taboos and prohibitions in other areas. Once you decide to stop thinking for yourself, you tend to do so in many other arenas.

Before moving into this chapter, take a second to examine how you think about sex and your experience of sex. How do you come to have the ideas, opinions, taboos, and desires you have? Are they of your own making or are they simply a reflection of a current or historical map-maker? Are they the result of a "cataclysmic" event you've chosen never to deal with or get over, or are they what seems a natural growth? A quick study of our personal sexual education may be important to get things rolling.

THE BELL CURVE

Almost all areas of life fall into a bell-shaped curve. Each end of the curve is the exception to the big bulge in the middle. Those with a very high IQ fall on one end, the very low on the other. With most things—IQ, athletic ability, reading, cooking, etc.—the general population falls somewhere in the large center. There are times when a category makes a shift and the bell gets skewed to one side or the other. A very cold winter will shift the normal range to one side, a specific population will have strengths that move the bell to the right or left. But in general, most things follow a rather standard Bell curve.

Sex is no different. Highly sexual on one end, non-sexual on the other. Sex, unlike things such as IQ that can be measured quantitatively, has no simple arithmetic. It is vastly different because of its qualitative variety and the subjective and social nature of it all. Homosexuality, group sex, S & M, pornography, etc. all have their own Bell curve, dependent yet largely independent of the sexual/non-sexual curve. With pornography there are degrees from soft porn to the most overt and explicit hard core. S & M ranges from light bondage to skin-tearing lashes. Each end of the curve has a small group of followers, with the bulk falling in the center. What makes it all so interesting and such an extraordinary smorgasbord is that this huge range of delectable differences allows anyone and everyone access to almost any outlet for their personal needs and desires.

Variety, space—the wonder of it all.

Unfortunately, many of these various Bell-shaped curves have been deemed taboo. Most of us secretly covet some of these other worlds and would love to spread our sexual wings and feel the heart of a new passion or the satisfaction of a repressed desire. We don't. We clandestinely window shop or chew on ice. We deny ourselves admission because at some point someone told us that "it" (you choose the "it") is not acceptable behavior. We bought it with no further exploration or questioning. We bind ourselves to a mast of denial that limits forays into mysteriously uncharted waters. In time, we may even refuse to allow ourselves flights of fantasy for fear of being lured close, then sucked into the vortex of "depravity," never again being able, or willing, to return. We learn to lie to ourselves, carefully fitting in with what someone else thought acceptable.

We bleach ourselves till we are white on the outside.

Our resentment (you know the word) grows. For some, self-denial can't hold out. They learn to live in hypocritical deception, lying to others about how deviant all "that" is while reveling in a secret "out of town" life of full participation and satisfaction.

Bleached white outside with a black core of deception. Finding desired experiences, but experiences tinged with lies, duplicity, hypocrisy, repeated as often as possible.

The deception grows. They lie to their partner about how they don't really want to play in another field or expand their sexual horizon, when indeed that is exactly what they want to do, and do.

Bleached white with a core of deceit.

In this world, there is no communication about sex outside the boundary of assumed mutual and proscribed consent. The subject just never comes up.

Bleached white with a hollow core.

The Champions of Sincerity stand guard over our standards of sexual behavior. They "chaz" and label as deviant any non-injurious sexual activity falling outside some arbitrary standards of conduct. Champions of Sincerity slavishly accept antique and bogus profiles of acceptability without the slightest insight or question as to "why." Through this myopic lens of judgment they condemn and limit not only others but themselves.

Their clarion call:

"Deviant is what I don't do!"

Sadly, their personal denial of variety and spice grows into deeper personal resentment that cannot be held in check. It can no longer be viewed as their own narrow prejudice. Champions of Sincerity proselytize. They become evangelical in their condemnation. With this evangelism they concoct a "higher ground" to set them above a world from which they have chosen to be excluded or that has not included them. Condemn, demean, repress, deny, imprison. All in the name of a "higher authority" with whom only they have communication.

How pathetic to believe such.

How demeaning to allow such.

The mill wheel of resentment grinds heavily upon the repressed erotic.

From this lofty "higher ground" the Champions of Sincerity wallow in their own exquisite form of sexual rapture ... self-flagellation, winning converts, large collection plates, towering cathedrals, fornication with a rough burlap robe on a cold night ... ecstasy and carnal pleasure in their own Bell curve.

It is from this position that these Champions of Sincerity inflict their *upright* rectitude on the unsuspecting and unwilling through "chazzing" and shallow recitation of unexamined and unquestioned moral dogmas. They sponsor or smile upon oppressive laws that deny others their benign individual rights to pursue their pleasure the way they choose. All is done in the name of a higher order. These guardians of the (temporal) moral code become corrupters of individual freedom. They gleefully spray their virulent and life-denying fumes behind closed doors and into darkened bedrooms to eradicate the evil.

Evil?

How can anything be evil if it produces no undesired pain? Is there any measure of evil other than the pain it brings? How can a moral code be moral if it eliminates pleasure that hurts no one? How can anyone deny another their pleasure if it has no impact on them and is agreed to by those concerned? There is no evil in agreed-to sexual activity. There is only evil in those trying to impose their restrictive morality on others. We should all learn who we are and not cover up our desire for an exceptional sexual life by condemning those who pursue theirs. It degrades the degrader.

So how do we come to better understand our own sensuality? How do we allow ourselves to dance in the vast fields of more enhancing and vibrant sexuality? How do we unshackle ourselves from our Victorian heritage and from the Champions of Sincerity? How do we stop lying to ourselves about erotic shoulds and shouldn'ts? How do we expand our experiences?

A few considerations I think are worth attention. You may not.

I do hope they will not be dismissed out-of-hand. Little should be dismissed that way.

1. Sex, with its vast permutations, is a delightful biological fact and is healthy.

    A. Sex alone is good.

    B. Sex with someone you like is better.

    C. Sex with someone you love is best.

    D. Sexlessness can be deviant and unhealthy.

A. Sex alone is good

Humans are sexual, as are most living things on earth. Humans are the only ones who pass judgment on what constitutes acceptable and unacceptable sexual behavior. For years masturbation was considered a taboo subject. It still is. We all found out how taboo when the U.S. Surgeon General tried to introduce it into the open American lexicon. She was hypocritically crucified and given the heave-ho. She did not lie. Everyone around her did. A simple fact: the vast majority of people masturbate. As many as 95% of males and 85% of females. Another simple fact: they like it. Another simple fact: they lie about it, and far too many try to impose that lie, their hypocrisy, their denial onto others. Few escape these sanctimonious hypocrites. The media pick up the topic because it's hot and controversial. From this media driven higher ground, the hypocrites suck the blood out of a universal activity, relegating it to a dark and taboo abnormality. The humor of it all is these hypocrites are sucking the blood out of themselves as they spend a few extra minutes in the bathroom telling themselves they are "relieving tension." They lie about it, but they judge.

Never listen to anyone who tells you there is anything bad about masturbation. Never tell anyone that it's wrong or will cause anything but pleasure. You will be lying and you will cause them to lie and miss an important experience in self-development. There are much more important things in your life than denying others. There are much better ways to live.

B. Sex with someone you like is better.

It's just more fun than alone. Two heads are better than one ... two steamy bodies are better than one. If you choose to have a sexual relationship with someone you like, try early to let each other know that it's nothing more than sex. Remember, sex is not love. The second you attach deep emotional baggage to this simple act of fun, the fun goes, the spontaneity is lost.

Don't misunderstand. Great friendships can and often do turn into something deeper. Great friendships that turn sexual are also dangerous. Let it flow but don't raise your level of expectation just because you've had sex. This is no easy task. We are programmed to seek, find and hold attachments. It assures the continuation of the species. But we are also, perhaps first and foremost, pleasure seeking creatures, and sex is a delightful if not the most delightful form of physical pleasure. If you choose to have sex with a friend, talk about it. Each partner needs to agree about what is expected and why you are choosing to move to the next step. If the communication is clear and ongoing, it can work. Be careful though. Most of the time communication fails and one person gets hurt. Sex is more powerful than a simple sentence in a book can ever express.

C. Sex with someone you love is best.

There is very little more to say.

D. Sexlessness can be deviant and unhealthy.

    1. Desire, too, follows the Bell-shaped curve.

Some people have no interest in sex. Although this lack of interest is a radical departure from the norm, it may not be wrong for that person. If the passion for an active sex life is missing in the genetic code, there is little one can do. If desire is missing for externally imposed reasons, then the acceptance of these impositions is unnatural and deviant. If you find yourself at odds with your passions and your actions, seek help. Coming to terms with your sexuality will open new doors that will indeed help you live like you mean it.

2. Sexual passion with one person tends to wane with time.
The challenge therefore is—to always keep it fresh and new. Never let your sexual relationship become stale because you and your partner are lazy. There is a world of erotica out there just waiting to be sampled. Get the books. Talk to friends. Learn. If you fail to do this when needed, expect a decline.

3. Don't lie about your sexual desires.
When you lie about your sexual desires, you lose and your partner loses. You lose because of the frustration you'll experience when compromising and denying. Frustration quickly turns to resentment when you are unwilling to risk trying or even suggesting new options for fear of rejection or accusation. "You've never wanted to do THAT before, what's come over you?" "Where did you ever come up with that idea? I have no intention of doing that!" "Who have you been talking to?" You have taught each other how to act and what to expect, but now you want to change the rules.

If your sex life if deadly dull, it needs changing. If you don't change it, you'll relegate it to a third or fourth place in your life and then you'll wonder why the gulf seems to grow with each day and night. The next step is *twin beds*.

4. The loss of sexual play is one hallmark of a moribund sexual relationship.
Relationships grow in a multitude of ways. Habits in relationships stop that growth. Habits become comfortable and seemingly secure. They are not. Sexual habits are no different. Think of the times you have heard of a "happy" couple who split for no apparent reason. Chances are the relationship had fallen into a comfortable habit that no one questioned. This habit was not only part of their daily life but their sexual life as well. Play at all levels.

5. Never attempt to or have sex with the unwilling or the defenseless … that's perversion and cruel.

6. Deviant sexual activity is deviant only to those not playing in that arena.
This is not to say there are not some deviant sexual activities, but if these activities do not violate the previous consideration, it may be difficult to prove.

7. The definition of pain and pleasure in sexual activity is subjective and should be left at that. The judgment is between those participating and not open to external evaluation or condemnation.

8. To judge someone else's sexuality is to confine yourself to a world with blinders.

The more you judge any activity (not just sex), the more entrenched you become in that judgment and the more pronounced your defense. Any orthodoxy hardens with defense. Back away; the only power that one should recognize is the power of a better judgment. That demands openness. Judgment stands with you and your partner. The rest is none of your business.

9. Never displace your sexual inadequacy onto others; that's resentment. Turn the resentment into improvement of yourself.

10. Reaction formation is very telling.
A study was conducted a number of years ago to explore the phenomena of gay bashing. There were two groups. The first, a group of "straight" men. The second, a group of homophobics. The groups were shown erotic films. During the films the arousal of all the participants was measured. The first film was heterosexual activity. During this film both groups were aroused, the "straight' men a bit more than the homophobic. The second film was homosexual activity. During the film the arousal of the "straight" man was very low. The arousal of the homophobic was higher, even higher than during the heterosexual film. Strange. "The lady protest too much me thinks."

11. Someone else's sexual activity is none of your business. There is no way this can be overstated.

Pursue pleasure, avoid pain. Is this one of the driving forces in a human? I think so. Is pleasure one criterion of a life worth reliving? I think so. Is sex one of the most pleasurable of human activities? I know so. It is surrounded with taboos and prohibitions that preclude full enjoyment? I know so. Can you change that?

If you choose.

Chapter 22
Elevating Experiences

We have spent a great deal of time discussing experiences and the critical and pivotal role they play in a life worth reliving. Now it's time to explore some specific aspects of experience to find and make the kind you want.

To start: There are two kinds of experiences:
First, happenstance. These are experiences that just happen to you. You're in the drug store and run into an old friend you haven't seen for years. You go to a coffee shop and spend a couple of hours in terrific conversation. Or, you take a wrong turn in a strange city and end up seeing delightful or awful things you never expected. These experiences come out of the blue with no thought or consideration on your part. These are almost always wonderful and there is no end to what they offer if you allow yourself to be swept away by them as opposed to viewing them as an inconvenience. Granted, when the event is not fun, this is not always easy to do, but remember you are in control of what you do about any situation. To wallow or not to wallow, that is the question. One choice yields little in the way of growth and acceptances of the hand life deals you. The other understands that every hand is not great but playing it the best you can is the only way to win.

The second kind of experience: planned. The ones you know are coming and for which you prepare. That trip to Greece next Sept. You have six months to read the books, study the maps, plan the itinerary, and talk to people. The wedding that makes you crazy for a year or so.

The parts of experience:
Every planned experience has three parts: the planning, the doing, and the remembering. For experiences of happenstance, two parts: the doing and the remembering. Let's explore a planned experience. It includes all three parts.

One thing, it's critical that even the most carefully planned experience should leave room for happenstance. The unintended might include an uninvited guest, the small fire, the unexpected phone call, the rain, the lady in the dark green dress. The intended, deciding to spend a night in a small hotel not on the agenda, talking to the couple at the next table, hopping on a boat going to the far side. These add a surprising dimension to an experience and can turn out to be the very best thing about the whole event. Granted, it can also be the pits, but don't let it take over. Ride it out with grace and flexibility. You never know, you might just discover America and not India.

To make the most of an experience all three parts should be considered as separate, although related. By looking at and using each part you'll enjoy each experience much more fully, in fact, three times more fully.

Elevating the experience:
All of us drift into experiences with little thought about the real importance they play in our lives. Another birthday. The experience rolls in, you let it happen, it rolls out, leaving you with only a vague remembrance that may or may not be worth repeating. What a pity.

How much better it would be if you could boost experiences to a new level, a level where each of the three parts, the planning, the doing, and the remembering had its own individual identity and magnitude? Wouldn't that be helpful in making an experience worth wanting to repeat?

Here's a way to get that ball rolling. Sit down alone, or with the person(s) with whom you will be sharing the experience. Pose the following "what if" questions. Have fun. Make sure each answer is directed toward the goal of wanting this (or any) experience you have one you would want to repeat.

Question 1

What if this will be the only time you will ever have this experience, and what if it will be the only experience you will ever remember?

Think about this. It's a one shot deal that will always be with you. You will never again be in a position to have this experience, or avoid remembering it. Exactly what would you do to make it outstanding? What would you bring to it to make sure it was the best single experience of your life?

Question 2

What if every experience were a direct reflection on and about you?

Assume this experience will be viewed by a great number of people and is the only way they and everyone in the world will ever see and judge you. How would you construct this experience so the reflection would be the one you really wanted, and one by which you would be willing to be judged?

Don't read this as simply accommodating what others think. Very much to the contrary. What you want is to project the image that will make the experience the best it can be for *you*. If you are going to a dinner party and you think it would enhance the experience to have people think of you in a new way, what would you do? How would you act? What image would you like to project? In short, what would you do to have the people at that party perceive you as you wanted to be perceived? How much more interesting and fun would it be if you took control of how others see you as opposed to letting them decide? This is in no way to imply that you will achieve the objective of making people see you the way you want. They may not. What you want and what will be fun is the challenge of trying to do that. The exciting thing about this idea is that the decision you make can be different with each event. A dinner, the theater, a blow-out party all offer a chance to establish the kind of image you want at those times and you think will provide you with the most memorable experience.

Add to this the simple fact that the way we see ourselves is often a reflection of the way others see and react to us. Our self-image doesn't stand alone, in very large part it grows from the reactions others have to us. If this dinner event were the only time we could affect that vision, how would we dress, act, think, and present ourselves so the reflection we got from others could be the one we thought interesting and important to us? In addressing this dinner party this way, you have elevated it to an interesting creative challenge and a chance to make it a worthy experience.

Question 3

What if this were an experience you could give to someone else? Someone you love very much. It will be his or her last experience and the only one they'll ever remember?

You have decided to take your grandmother to Paris. She is 88 and always wanted to make this trip. What would you do? What kind of hotel would you choose? Would you go for the luxury or the small, very French, hotel up on Montmartre? Would you eat at an American fast food joint or find a delightful cafe overlooking the Eiffel Tower and the Seine? How far would you be willing to go to make this the most fantastic time in Grandma's life?

Treat yourself like your grandmother.

Go back and review the three elevating questions. As you study them, don't let the example restrict your thinking. Replace the dinner with a trip to the grocery store. How bout shopping in the gourmet section for something you've never bought or made? A city council meeting. Get on the agenda with you pet park project and include three or four people looking for the same thing. Your next date. Think of the Monster Truck event you have never attended. The more focus and life you give to the questions, the more interesting and exciting your ideas.

The worth of most experiences is up to you if you choose to take control and use your imagination.

The components:

Think again about the three components of experience, the planning, the doing, and the remembering. Apply the three experience elevating questions to each of these three parts. If you were off to

London and you knew it would be the only time you would ever be able to go, how much effort would you put in the planning, the doing, and then the remembering? If you wanted the folks in London to view you in a special way, how would you plan to act, dress, etc? What would you do while there that might make the desired impression? How would you want to remember the trip?

The Planning:

Don't just plan the trip, make the planning an event unto itself. Get the maps and study them as if you will never really make the trip and that the study is the experience. If you are going to a party, think about how you'll dress to reflect the exact image you want. Go to the store and look at the dress and envision how you'll look. Is it a knock'em dead dress or just ho hum? Go into the dressing room and imagine how everybody will look at you and how you'll feel when you enter in that short little black dress. Take your husband or significant other into the dressing room with you. That's even more fun. How bout some really sexy lingerie? How does it make you feel? Would it be fun sitting there next to the big shot preacher knowing you have on that black thong or a brand new push-up bra? (This may just be a male fantasy but if it's the topic of conversation before the dinner it may be great fun for both of you at the dinner). Are you having fun planning? If you aren't it's your own fault, and you can do something about it.

Another way to enjoy the planning is to elevate the event in your mind. A simple political meeting can become a rally if you choose. Play with it. Let the prospect of a dynamic revolution capture you. Don't just settle for another dull afternoon, make it an event. Your objective is to make the planning just as important to the experience as the doing and remembering. If the meeting turns out to be just another meeting, at least you had a lot of fun planning.

The Doing:

The operative word is "gusto". Once you are in the event, be in the event one hundred percent. It's so easy to sit back and not go to the dance floor that everything passes in a dull haze. All you're left with is a party that took place a few weeks ago with nothing worth recalling. Granted, not all events will be scintillating. Some will just sit there like a dead fish. That doesn't excuse you from finding something in it worth remembering or doing. Think back to the experience elevating questions. What if this was the last event you would ever attend? What would you do? The event doesn't care if you have a bad or memorable evening. You do and it's up to you to make it so.

If you were going to repeat this event, how would you change it to make it more enjoyable? You can do that right in the middle of the event, if you choose.

The Remembering:
Like the planning and the doing, the remembering should have a life of its own. As nearly as possible, the experience of remembering an event should be as much fun as the event itself. Often this is really easy to do. Reading a diary and looking at the photos of a trip to Rome on a cold rainy day back home can be fraught with as much excitement as actually walking into the Coliseum. A video of your first solo flight can conjure up a host of feelings and remembrances of the anxiety you felt when the instructor told you to take it around, alone.

If the idea of experience is to make it as well-rounded as you can, then keeping copious notes or drawings of the event well add a sparkling dimension to remembering.

An example:
Not long ago my delicious partner, Jill, and I were invited to a party. This was not just a party, it was a dress-up party. It was held at a posh place with people we didn't know. The dress was casual but fun and, if we chose, sexy. It was about that time that I was writing this chapter so I thought we might practice by really working on the three aspects of an experience.

My first question to Jill, how do we want to present ourselves to this group so we can enjoy the experience and the experience of them experiencing us? Or, how do we want to be reflected? Also, how could we make this the kind of experience that, if it were the last one, we would be delighted to remember it?

Our planning was great fun. We looked through her closet

(men's clothes don't matter a whole lot, we all look pretty much the same in dark suits) and decided which was the most interesting, and closest to the edge (perhaps the very place to be on any occasion). Since we knew only a few people at the party we thought we could push the envelope and make if fun for us and present an "interesting" persona to the group.

We talked about how we would involve ourselves with new people and how we would be more assertive in making introductions. We discussed how we would find out more about the other guests, determined to leave with a few new friends. The whole planning process took a couple of hours over several days.

In the spirit of planning, I took the car to the car wash and had a fine time thinking about what we had discussed and how much fun we were going to have. Later, we had a great time getting all dressed up and ready.

Looking back, we agreed that the planning stood alone and was a major part of the entire event.

When we walked in the door, we were clearly "unique". There were only a few people and not at all what we expected. Most were dressed in what looked like their work clothes and had made no special preparation for the event. Everyone seemed to be just milling about and not engaging or apparently having a very good time, asleep on the hay wagon, as it were. We looked at each other, smiled, and went ahead with our plan. She went one way, I another. We made introductions and asked some leading, open ended questions. The introductions went well but the leading questions yielded little worth perusing. After about an hour, we managed to meet back on a sofa. We took a seat, looked at each other and started to laugh. Nothing we expected had come about. We had expected the group to be something it turned out not to be.

As we sat there we started looking around the room. There was an old stone wall someone had fixed up very nicely. We studied the wall and talked about the stones, where they came from, how old they were. We then speculated on the person who had done the work. When had he done it. What tools did he used? What was his life like at the time? We had just finished taking a course on ancient

Egypt so we compared the work. This speculation became a great game that enhanced the event. There was even an old lava lamp on a table in the corner that became a great topic of discussion and humor. Pretty soon we were having a wonderful time just looking around, watching the people and taking in the room. What we had decided to do was turn the initial expectation into a different reality and just enjoy this new reality.

We stayed at the party for almost four hours and did indeed have some good conversations with a few late arrivals. We headed back to the hotel and spent a great night laughing and giggling with each other about the plan and the reality.

Driving home the next day we talked about the evening. The conversation was delightful and although the party was not what we expected, we found ways to make it a memorable experience. Was it one we would repeat? Probably not. Would we erase it from our memory? No way, the parts were way too much fun.

Some final thoughts:

Don't try to elevate every experience to the highest point possible. That would take far too much effort and time. It would also be impossible. Some experiences just happen and they assume no meritorious position in the archives of your memory. That's all right. If every experience were so elevated, there would be no contrast with experiences of less quality. Contrast is the key to all enjoyment. Choose, but choose often.

Each experience is what it is or what you decide to make it. The three parts: the planning, the doing, and the remembering each can be fashioned into something worth remembering individually. We had a great time planning our party, and the less than fabulous event took nothing away from that.

The key is to be flexible and not compare one event to another or be disappointed that it doesn't meet the level of expectation randomly set by you. Once you start comparing, nothing will ever really assume its own place in your memory. It will always lack. I have a friend from New York who always compares what she does here to the way it's done in the city. She never squeezes the most out of the here and now. Always tell yourself that this is this, and that is that. They are not supposed to be the same. Instant coffee is instant coffee and *not* fresh ground. They are not meant to be the same and if all you do is compare, little will meet your expectation. Little will be an experience worth repeating.

This doesn't mean you should not be discriminating. You should indeed be discriminating. Discrimination is a large part of what makes you you. Discrimination should come in evaluating the thing itself, not strictly in the comparison. Do you like this for what it is? How would you change it to make it better in and of itself? You may use the knowledge gained from other experiences but that knowledge should not be an immutable standard, only a guide. There is far too much fear of stepping out of the "accepted" boundaries. The scrumptious apple pie you had at a small cafe may tell you that you need more cinnamon in your pie, but you are adding it because you like the addition, not because you want simply to replicate that pie. Your creativity should always expand what you already know or do. Repetition is for machines. Move beyond. Far beyond.

Also, watch for habits. The poison of a habit is insidious. The same friends, the same restaurant, the same vacation will numb or kill the best in you. Look for the new, or look at what is familiar with fresh eyes. Your field of vision has much less to do with the field than with the eyes viewing the field. Turn things you know around to look at them in a different way. We are much more attracted to the new and are often, unknowingly, repelled by the same old thing. With a bit of searching and creativity, even the most mundane can become the exciting. Have you ever made love on your washer during the spin cycle? Or taken a new way home? Or looked at your world through the eyes of a visitor? No? Too bad.

Repeatable experiences! That's the objective, isn't it?

⧗

Chapter 23

Sand, Water, Oil and the Arizona

Luxor, Egypt.

I sit in The Great Hypostyle Room in the Temple of Karnak, a wonder of the ancient or any world. I've been here for four hours. The mammoth columns that make up this room are overwhelming. I study the hieroglyphics hoping to understand anything about the people who carved them, their message to the priests and pharaohs that walked the stone paths, and the message to us in the post-modern world. For a second my mind races back to the Jain temple high over steamy Bombay. What connects the years and miles between these places? What happened to those who walked in these temples? Where are they now? Who were the carvers? How are we supposed to remember the mythological people for whom the carvers carved? What happened to all of them as the sand passes thorough the narrow neck of the unbiased hourglass? What is the link? What is the use? Is there a connection or a use to us? Is it important or simply a stroll down an antique memory lane?

I sit and think.

The sun in upper Egypt is kiln hot. The sandy desert on the far side of the Nile shimmers with silver waves of ersatz water. I think of Shelley's Ozymandias.

> *I met a traveler from an antique land*
> *Who said: "Two vast and trunkless legs of stone*
> *Stand in the desert. Near them, on the sand,*

Half sunk, a shattered visage lies, whose frown,
And wrinkled lip, and sneer of cold command,
Tell that its sculptor well those passions read
Which yet survive, stamped on these lifeless things,
The hand that mocked them, and the heart that federal:
And on the pedestal these words appear:
`My name is Ozymandias, king of kings:
Look on my works, ye Mighty, and despair!'
Nothing beside remains. Round the decay
Of that colossal wreak, boundless and bare
The lone and level sands stretch far away."

I studied this poem in college and now clearly recall its words as I watch the ancient sands of the Hypostyle Room lift in errant swirls from a time worn floor. My professor said the poem was about man's pathetic and useless quest to find immortality locked away in rocks and carvings. Quest that proved futile even to the great Ozymandias whose trunkless legs of stone lay toppled over in sullen anticipation of wind, sand, and time exacting their final toll. At the time I thought he was correct, and that this poem was really about the vanity of those efforts in imperishability. About how nothing stays. About how the things we build all fall down and are eventually covered in a blanket of sand, humus, sea, historical neglect, and obscuring time.

I no longer agree.

I don't think Shelley was telling us about the meaninglessness of Ozymandias's life and his futile attempt to net and capture eternity. He knew that couldn't be done. Nothing stays. The webbing of a temporal capture net is fully permeable to anything synonymously past, present, and future. Entropy prevails. We now know that in some distant and apathetic epoch our sun will go nova and a sparkling white-hot morning will dawn. At that scorching moment the lush green of the land and the deep blue seas melt away. The great library fire of Alexandria will be worldwide and the noble and ignoble works of man will drift skyward in black irretrievable smoke and ash. The time that we measure, the time that now so methodically regulates our days, vanishes leaving only a dry shell with hot winds blowing from nowhere to nowhere, measured by no one. At the far end, the heat fades and an endless cold moves in. Our verdant home becomes a dark cinder drifting in a void with no intention, no conclusion. The story is over.

Ozymandias and Shelley both knew this so why just report it? They were both far above such a simple observation.

Diagnosis is not prescription.

Perhaps Shelley was after something else, something much grander, more immediate. Maybe he was asking a question: "Where is your monument toppled over and exfoliating in the lone and level desert sand? Where are your hieroglyphics? What did you make in your time? What speaks of you?" Shelley and the great Ozymandias both knew that the glacial disappearance of a stone statute is only a passing consideration; nothing compared to the imperishable void left by those who have never carved anything.

How do you read the poem?

A Dark Sea and a Change of Pace

The *Tropic Rover*, a one hundred fifty-foot catamaran at sea, at midnight fighting a raging gale just off Nassau.

I stand at the wheel in a strenuous but useless attempt to steer a worthy course. The ship is backing into a potential disaster. Hours earlier the sea was calm, puffy white clouds drifting in a sea blue sky that met the horizon in an unbroken line. All that changed and we must all deal with it.

The mid-night wind picks up even more. The skipper orders me down to the bow to hang the anchors ... a seemingly useless maneuver when backing into a coral reef. Nothing else was working. The jib had blown out and we had not been able to reef the staysal. To hang the anchor required going down almost to water level and unhooking a small rope holding the anchor up between the two hulls. I look at the skipper. The waves were crashing up over the deck and to hang the anchors required going to a level below the decks. This was not the military, I did not have to do this. I went. I struggled my way to the bow and told the first mate what the skipper wanted done. He looked at me. I looked back and headed to the catwalk spanning the hulls.

A mid-night sea during a gale is a dark place. The only light interrupting the dark was one small spot next to the winch. This light illuminated the void between the two hulls. It was into this void I had to go. The halo of light on the water was only about fifteen feet wide. With the approach of each wave the circle grew small and then expanded as the crest plunged into a trough. Past the small penumbral edge of the light, blackness extended into an imaginary world of sea creatures, galleons, and denizens that interrupt soothing sleep.

I held tight to the catwalk as I inched toward the small rope that held the anchor. At an uneven pace dark green monsters rose from the black and washed over me forcing me back against the rail. I tightened my grip on the cold steel. The wave would pass and I would inch again toward my goal. I could hear Roy, the first mate, yelling to me that another wave was coming. I would brace and take it head on.

A break between the waves. I reached up and lifted the small rope from around the shank of the anchor then braced myself again for another assault.

I inched back to the ladder and away from the anchor now being lowered into the green. About half way back I stopped. I watched a green aquatic monster build, swallow me then spit me out into a hollow valley of heightened expectation. I stopped and waited for another wave to emerge from the black night. Roy yelled for me to get back. I paused.

The change from the small light to the dark interior of the wave: remarkable. The change from the deep trough between the weaves to the towering crest; remarkable. The change between the puffy white clouds of the morning and the howling wind and pounding sea at night; remarkable. The change a few hours later from a howling sea to flat water; remarkable.

Change. How remarkable.

Change, the only constant. It's random, or at best guided. Never fully directed; too many wild cards stack the deck. Change has its own agenda. It comes full force, in your face, or as an un-expected gale from a calm day. The best we can hope for is that the agenda be kind, allowing some gentle pushing, flights of ex treme luck (most of which you make), and an indulgent yielding to a determined will. Expecting more is foolish, debilitating, and agonizing.

There are, however, three critical words that may prove advantageous in helping guide change and tame the errant winds that sweep us up and deposit us in unexpected and unpredictable land-scapes. One proviso: even with a thousand words, never believe you fully control your world. Attempting to do so will endlessly frustrate you and preclude the enjoyment blossoming form happenstance and random encounters. Let the mystery, both tragic and delectable, lace your days of change with wonder and an essential understanding that neither tragedy or delectability lasts, take both as they come and as simply the way it is.

The first word, attitude.

What is your attitude toward the world? Never forget, the world has no attitude toward you. It's totally dispassionate, apathetic, cold. You, and all before you are perishable spores with a very short tenure. You, and you alone choose your attitude and, ergo, your view of the world. If you think the impassive world is for you or against you, owes you a living or denudes your resources, you are ascribing far more importance to yourself than you deserve. You just aren't that important. The world cares not a whit about you and your brief little moment of existence. How could it? Your care and your attitude determine the smoothness or rockiness of your road.

So, what is your attitude? Is it open or closed? Does it allow a full spectrum of experiences or rigorously edit them in light absorbing fear, prejudice, preconceived notions, dogma, and rigid bigotry? Does it embrace the new, the unique, and the unexpected or does it believe what "they" say? Does it tuck its head under the cover and hide? If your attitude is rigid and closed, you'll be swimming against the tide of change that inevitably sweeps around, over and through all of us. It's an aquatic battle you will lose. When the tide ebbs you will be left on a dry sandy beach with all the others gasping for interesting air and wondering about all the fascinating things that swim in the sea from which you have removed yourself. On the other hand, if your attitude is open, accepting, exploratory, and curious the tide will move you into new and often delightful pools of calm and tempestuous rapids that add dramatic dimensions to your days. Your aquatic adventure will by amniotic as opposed to traumatic and the inevitable vicissitudes of existence will crash you more gently on the rocks and shoals.

Explore your attitudes. Are they life-affirming or life-denying? Step back. Explore life-affirming and life-denying as objectively as you can. Ask others what they find life-affirming and life-denying. Don't filter their response through your eyes. Listen with the third ear, the one that lets in the new stuff. If your attitude is open, so is the world. If your attitude is rigidly orthodox, fundamental, dogmatic, so is your world. The world isn't that rigid. It doesn't work that way. It's a kaleidoscope, of color, not a canvas of black and white.

Let your attitude reflect the remarkably varied way of the world. If it doesn't, adjust your attitude. Don't expect the world to. It won't.

The next word is circumstance.

Life is circumstance. The circumstances into which you are thrown, the circumstances that befall you, and finally the circumstances you make. Circumstances always change. Things happen, or you make things happen. Either way, it's in the circumstances of your life that you exercise your attitude. It's also in your attitude and passions that you create many of your circumstances.

An interesting and pregnant interplay of action/reaction.

Act in concert with circumstances as they befall you. Master the art of accommodating and creating life-affirming circumstances. Push gently. Manipulate as prudent. Don't battle, you won't win. Depart from given circumstances if they aren't working. Believe you can do that and don't let history or bogus obligations sway your desire. Never forget that in departing from one set of circumstances, you take yourself with you. Be sure that you are a worthy travel companion. If not, assess the kind of person with whom you would like to travel and work to become that person. Otherwise, the abandoned circumstances will reappear with a new face and the journey will end in a familiar cul-de-sac. Vast sums of unsalvageable time will have been squandered. There is no time for that.

Like the world, circumstances don't care. You do. It's in that passionate caring that you adjust your attitude to create the kind of circumstances important to a life worth re-living.

That is the point, isn't it?

The last of the three words: Opportunity.

The rooms of attitude and circumstances are filled with a vast number of doors. No matter which direction you turn, there is a door waiting. The more open and accepting your attitude, the more interesting and challenging your circumstances, the better the quality of the adventure behind the doors. The more restrictive, the more vanilla.

At any moment in our life you face the option of turning the handle to one of these doors yourself, or having the door open of its own accord. Doors open, and that's that. you can never stay in the same room for any extended time. The world doesn't work that way. Things change. You will move from room to room as circumstances dictate. If the best you can muster is a passive passage into what seems a safe and understood room then you are not seizing an opportunity to take control. You are a passenger, sleeping on the hay wagon. You deserve the numbing repetition that lies in wait behind the open door. If, on the other hand, you heed the knocking at the closed door, take the risk of answering, then take the risk of entering, you become the driver of the hay wagon and the ride assumes a direction. The choice could prove disastrous. There is a risk either way. Most likely you'll find a delightful and challenging world of unique adventures and life-affirming experiences.

Remember, opportunity doesn't care whether you seize it or let it silently pass by. Why should it? Opportunity doesn't care whether you answer the knock or whether you turn a fearful deaf ear. Why should it? You and you alone care if you reach for the brass knob.

Let the others sleep. Your world is knocking.

Afternoon. Pearl Harbor.

I am standing a few feet above the rusting hulk of the battleship

Arizona. The day is exceptional. The water clear. Under my feet rest hundreds of men trapped below deck in the morning attack. I look down through the water at the rusting reminder. From time to time small drops of oil from the ship's fuel tanks bubble up and form tiny explosions on the surface.

These eruptions spread into a glimmering pattern on the surface then slowly dissipate into the vast sea. For a moment I think of each drop as the essence of one of the men who died during the attack. The shining pattern of the oil forms a momentary Rorschach of their life. A Rorschach quickly lost forever in the ripple of tide, wind, and time. Each drop, for a second, has its own luster and changing form. Each drop has its unique place in that momentary and mysterious little universe of the sea, the time, and the bright sun. It's time finished, it disappears and is replaced by another drop that assumes its own form and color. A process in a process that has no meaning above and beyond the meaning we each give it in our shining moment on the surface of the sea.

It is in that momentary bubbling to the surface that we find ourselves thrown into the world as aesthetically conscious beings. It is that momentary time of glimmering on the surface that we become responsible for the shape and luster of our existence. It is in that mysterious conjunction of elements that all we are is manifest.

It is a wonderful story that only you can tell.

Epilogue

Twilight at the Valley of the Kings on the West Bank of the Nile. The night sky. More thinking.

I lean back on the still warm sand and look deep into the evolving darkness of the Egyptian sky. My mind races to "those" questions. They're not new, I have asked them hundreds of times: on a ship in the middle of the Atlantic, on a side-wheeler on the misty Congo River, in the open desert of Arizona, on a roof top in Zanzibar, at the edge of the pounding sea in Nova Scotia. They're the questions surrounding my complete ignorance in the face of understanding the terrestrial abyss, the stars and the midnight void between it all. Tonight, on a hill in a land stretching back to the edge of man's history, I ask them again. Where does it begin? How did it begin? How did it get here? Where does it end? Why am I here now and not somewhere else in another time? What is the point? Tonight, however, is different. I have an answer: The questions don't matter. What does matter is what you do and how you live. What is the special song you are supposed to be singing? Only you can write the melody. Only you can write the words. Only you can stand up and sing the song. It's all an enchanting solo act played in concert with all that have come before and all that are on stage with you now. Find enchantment in all of it, the good, the bad, the unknown and the unknowable. Be big-hearted in your attitude. Do the right thing because it makes you feel good, not because some external force tells you to. Extortion has no longevity, big-heartiness does.

Believe in an afterlife if you choose, but don't let the promise of that life preclude full involvement in this. They can exist in concert. Let no one tell you different.

Have a great time as your small drop of oil appears on the surface of this shining sea.

It dissipates far too quickly.

What is remembered after a wind storm...

...often only the wind, not the twigs and paper flying about in the melee. Books are no different. What is remembered is a wind of the words, seldom the full content. Content fades. This book too will prove no different.

There is, however, something specific I would like you to try to remember if not memorize. Something I hope will stick with you, haunt you, drive you, lift you. Read carefully. Understand when the poet says "you", he means *you*.

Enivrez-vous
(Get Drunk)
by Charles Baudelaire

You must always be drunk. Everything is there: it is the only question. Not to feel the horrible burden of Time breaking your shoulders and bowing you toward the earth, you must get drunk without stopping.

But on what? On wine, on poetry, or on virtue, after your fashion. But get drunk.

And if sometimes, on the steps of a palace, in the green grass of a ditch, in the dreary solitude of your own room, you wake up, with your drunkenness already lessened or gone, as wind, wave, star, bird, clock, everything that flees, murmurs, sings, rolls, speaks, ask what time is it; and wind, wave, star, bird, clock, will answer you: 'It is time to get drunk!' Not to be the tormented slave of Time, get drunk without stopping! On wine, on poetry, or on virtue, after your fashion.